FRENCH ARMY
REGIMENTS AND UNIFORMS
from the Revolution to 1870

1. *Imperial Guard Chasseurs à cheval, 1804–1815 (see page 22)*

FRENCH ARMY REGIMENTS AND UNIFORMS

from the Revolution to 1870

by

W. A. THORBURN

London: Arms and Armour Press
New York: Hippocrene Books, Inc.

Published by
Arms and Armour Press
Lionel Leventhal Limited
2–6 Hampstead High Street,
London NW3 1PR
© W. A. Thorburn, 1969
Reprinted 1976
All rights reserved

ISBN 0 85368 241 0

Published in the United States, 1976
by Hippocrene Books, Inc.,
171 Madison Avenue,
New York, N.Y. 10016

ISBN 0–88254–411–X

LC 76–13825

To MM. Jean Brunon and Paul Martin who encouraged my
early studies of the French army and to my mentor and friend
Mr. A. E. Haswell Miller who introduced me to print collecting.

Printed Offset Litho in Great Britain by
Cox & Wyman Ltd, London, Fakenham and Reading

Contents

2. *Hussars, 1810 (see page 74)*

The French Army

French military power was always a major factor in the affairs of Europe as a whole.

It influenced all aspects of military thought throughout the world. No discussion on warfare or army organisation can be carried on without frequent use of French language terms, and by the mid-19th century, nearly every land force in the world wore at least a version of French uniform.

The earliest records of regularly paid troops in France are those of the 15 companies of men-at-arms raised by Charles VII in 1444. The most senior Infantry regiments can trace their lineage to the 16th century, and the Cavalry were formed into regiments by Louis XIV.

Guard regiments were the first to wear distinctive dress, but a more general use of uniform clothing did not occur until 1670, and even then this was mainly confined to foreign units in the French service. By about 1690, however, all infantry were issued with coats of a grey-white colour, while the mounted troops wore a variety of shades.

During the 18th century white was the standard colour for Line Infantry. This was not as spectacular as might be imagined however, since this was the colour of the coarse undyed wool that was used, dyed cloth, apart from distinctive cuffs and collars, being reserved for the Guards, Cavalry and foreign corps.

One has only to mention the names of Turenne, Condé and Saxe to be reminded of the deeds of the French Army before the Revolution, but it is the soldiers of the First Republic and Empire who make the most lasting impression on the mind and eye. These were the men who shook Europe to its foundations, at a time when purely martial designs were replacing the modified civilian clothing of the 18th century. They were not only demonstrating a new kind of warfare, but also were beginning to appear in the elegant and characteristic styles for which France was to become famous.

Shortly before the end of the Old Régime there were in the Army 134,236 Infantry, 29,586 Cavalry and 77,692 Militia or Provincial Troops, with an additional 8,560 men in the Royal Household. This force, although at first confused, did not disappear, and it was the trained existence of the old regiments which served as a basis for the new armies of the Republic. The uniforms regulated by the Royal Order of 21st February 1786 continued in use for as long as they were wearable, and these styles survived in the cavalry up to the Consulate. The new clothing regulations of the Empire from 1804 were a continuation and development of the 1786 fundamentals.

The Empire and its instruments died on 18th June 1815, but the French Army did not, and by 1818 it consisted of 119,895 men, increasing to 164,326 in the following year. In 1823 the restored monarchy was invading Spain with an army of 115,855 men, and in 1828, 13,378 out of a total of 308,796, were in Greece.

The white Bourbon flags went on campaign for the last time to Algeria, and in 1830 Louis Philippe, son of the Duke of Orléans, became King of the French. The conquest of Algeria was carried through under his Gallic Cock standards, and so began the Army's long connection with North Africa.

The strength at this period was 389,273 men, 31,330 of whom were in Algeria, and in 1833 the numbers had risen to 410,000. Voluntary enlistment is not normally associated with continental armies, but between 1820 and 1830 an average of 8,600 Frenchmen volunteered annually—about one-seventh of the total recruited.

French troops were in Belgium in 1831, in Mexico during 1838 and 1839, and in addition to actions in Algeria they extended their activities to Morocco in 1844.

In 1848 the Orléans Monarchy was deposed, and until 1851 the country was ruled by a Provisional Republican Government, which, other than tinkering with insignia, did nothing to change the basic organisation of the army, which was soon fighting in Italy. In 1849 the brazen notes of the field music echoed through the streets of Rome, and the Infantry of the Line tramped in dressed according to the Regulations of 1845, their strutting *vivandières* being remarked on unfavourably by staid English residents.

After a brief period as President of the Republic, Louis Napoleon, nephew of Napoleon Bonaparte, was created Emperor in 1852 with the title of Napoleon III. (Bonaparte's son, the possible Napoleon II, had died in 1832.) Paris was once again the capital of an Empire, tall grenadiers in bearskin caps stood on guard at the Tuileries, and the Army was to be the most brilliant symbol of a new age of elegance. The bourgeois boredom of the previous régime was forgotten, and the eagles on shakos and standards proclaimed that the great days had returned. As was to be clear 18 years later, this was a myth, but the dark clouds were far away.

In the early years of the new Empire, French troops fought

alongside British soldiers in the Crimea, and whereas the gallant British Army struggled to do its duty in spite of overwhelming incompetence, the French created a deep impression of professionalism. When the *4th Chasseurs d'Afrique* swept down in mounted skirmishing order to sabre astounded Russian gunners who were playing havoc with the ill-fated Light Brigade, they did much not only to help their unaccustomed comrades-in-arms, but also to emphasise the disparity between the two armies.

After the Crimean War British uniforms became totally French in design, and all over the world the rakish *képi* was the standard military headgear.

The War with Austria in 1859 placed the seal on belief in French military superiority and the victories at Solferino and Magenta were compared with Wagram and Austerlitz. The *Chasseurs à pied* and *Zouaves* carried all before them, but it was a legend feeding on itself and the soldiers, by their bravery in the field, were helping their Emperor to play out his pretence of Imperial greatness.

While the war between the States raged in America a French army of 45,000, plus two battalions of the Foreign Legion, were in Mexico. At first the men of Magenta and Africa made short work of the opposition, but too soon the country and the cause turned sour and after years of frustrating and fruitless work by the army, the adventure was ended and the tragic Maximilian was left to his fate in 1867. All that remained was perhaps the legend of the 3rd Company of the 1st Foreign Legion, who were to remain for ever at the immortal village of Camerone.

The stage was now set for the great *débacle* of 1870, and the splendid regiments of the last French Empire were to discover that Prussians were not Austrians, nor were they the same Prussians who had been swept aside in the time of that other Empire. The proud columns faltered, broke and were cut down, or were herded into masses without plan or hope of escape. Paris had to be defended by the people themselves, following the failure of the army that once had been a model for all.

With that remarkable French genius for recovery a new Republican Army was created out of the wreckage, and pride in past achievements revived. This was the army that, in all the panache of red trousers and blaring bugles, flung itself on the Germans in 1914, stood firm at Verdun in steel helmet and horizon blue, and bled to death for Nivelle in 1917.

Governments came and went, Kings and Emperors rose and fell. The French soldier, however, too often betrayed, or sacrificed for political expediency, has a firm place in the pages of history and we should know what he looked like, and something about the regiments he served in.

Between the early 19th century and the 1860s, engravings and lithographs were a popular source of pictorial information, a feature being the production of sets, or individual prints, showing soldiers and their various uniforms.

Such prints, published at the time, or from the work of artists who had actually seen the subjects depicted, are a major source of historical information, and a selection of those dealing with French uniforms are used here.

The Kings, Emperors, and Governments of France were served by very numerous auxiliary, temporary, colonial, and foreign troops, but these are not discussed in detail, and are only mentioned where their existence touches on Guard or Line organisation of the regular French Army.

3. *Horse Artillery, 1810*

The Royal Artillery was the 64th Regiment in the infantry list, but a separate corps of Horse Artillery was raised in 1792.

By 1830 mobile mounted batteries were also included in field regiments, and during the Second Empire only five out of the twenty regiments were Foot Artillery.

10

Royal and Imperial Guards

The old *Maison du Roi* or Household Troops disappeared after the Revolution, but on 30th September 1791 the National Assembly created a force of Foot and Horse called *Garde Constitutionelle du Roi*, which was however disbanded in May 1792 as unreliable.

The senior regiment of the old Monarchy was the *Gardes Françaises*, which had been disbanded in 1789, the men going to make up the National Guard of Paris. In August 1791 they were absorbed into the 102nd, 103rd and 104th Regiments of the Line. Some also went to the *Gendarmerie*.

On 15th May 1791 men from the old *Gendarmerie Royale* were formed into a *Garde de l'Assemblée Nationale*, the same corps being renamed the *Garde de la Convention* on 30th September 1792. In 1793 it consisted of one battalion of 500 men, with one company of Grenadiers, later in the year augmented by a battery of artillery. The title was again changed, this time to *Garde du Corps Legislatif*, and on 11th November 1799 it amalgamated with the *Garde du Directoire* to become the Consular Guard. By 1802 the Consular Guard consisted of two battalions of Grenadiers, and two of *Chasseurs*, with eight companies each. There were also four squadrons of Horse Grenadiers, four of *Chasseurs à cheval*, and a unit of Artillery. On 29th July 1804 these units became the senior regiments of the new Imperial Guard created by Napoleon. Two squadrons of *Gendarmes d'Élite* also shared this distinction.

The Imperial Guard infantry regiments normally had eight companies, and the cavalry four to five squadrons, but these varied from time to time.

The regiments of the Imperial Guard were as follows:—

Imperial Guard (*Foot*)

Grenadiers à pied—1st Regiment 1804, 2nd 1806. These were amalgamated in 1808 and a new 2nd Regiment was formed in 1811.
Grenadiers Hollandais—incorporated in 1810 as 2nd Regiment. Later numbered 3rd on raising of the 2nd French Regiment.
Pupilles (*Hollandais*)—nine battalions in 1811, reduced to two in 1813, the other battalions going to form the *Tirailleurs* and *Voltigeurs*.
Fusiliers-Grenadiers—raised in 1806, disbanded 1814.
Tirailleurs-Grenadiers—raised in 1809, called *Tirailleurs* from December 1810.

Conscrits-Grenadiers—raised in 1809, became 3rd and 4th *Tirailleurs* in 1811.

Tirailleurs—(from 1811).

Flanqueurs-Grenadiers—raised 1811 with two battalions.

Chasseurs à pied—raised in 1804 from the Consular Guard with a 2nd Regiment raised in 1806.

Fusiliers-Chasseurs—raised in 1806, disbanded in 1814.

Tirailleurs-Chasseurs—raised in 1809 with two battalions. Became *Voltigeurs* in 1810.

Conscrits-Chasseurs—raised in 1809, its two regiments became 3rd and 4th *Voltigeurs* in 1811.

Voltigeurs—19 regiments—7th from *Garde Nationale de la Garde*, 14th, 15th and 16th with *Garde Royale d'Espagne*.

Flanqueurs-Chasseurs—raised in 1813.

Vélites—raised in 1804. Two companies attached to the *Grenadiers* and two to the *Chasseurs à pied*. (*Vélites* were also attached to some of the Cavalry of the Guard, but these were abolished in 1811, except those with the 2nd Lancers of the Guard.)

Ouvriers d'Administration (302 men in three companies)—raised in 1806 as *Service d'Administration de la Garde Impériale,*—*bouchers, botteleurs, infirmiers, train des ambulances.*

Imperial Guard (Cavalry)

Grenadiers à cheval—from Consular Guard (five squadrons). Ranked with Foot Grenadiers as senior.

Gendarmes d'Élite—from *Gendarmes d'Élite* of Consular Guard 1804. Two squadrons.

Gendarmes d'Ordonnance—disbanded 1807. (Actually served mostly on foot.)

Chasseurs à cheval (Old Guard)—from 1804 from Guides of Consular Guard. Five squadrons to nine squadrons in 1814.

2nd *Chasseurs à cheval* (Young Guard)—raised in 1815 largely from the conscripts who had formed the 9th Squadron of the 1st Regiment.

Mamelukes—a company attached to the *Chasseurs à cheval* from 1804, raised to a squadron in 1813.

Dragons (*Dragons de l'Impératrice*)—called Empress's Dragoons from 1807.

Chevau-Légers-Polonais (1st and 3rd)—the 3rd was raised in 1812, but was incorporated with the 1st from 1813.

Chevau-Légers-Lanciers (2nd Regiment)—from 1810 (*Lanciers Rouges*). The Lancers of the Guard were all *Chevau-Legers-Lanciers*, Regiments 1, 2 and 3. The 1st and 3rd were Polish, the 2nd Dutch and French.

12

Lanciers de Berg—Murat's *Chasseurs à cheval* from the Grand-Duché de Berg, from 1809 *Lanciers de Berg*. They passed to the service of Prussia on the dissolution of the Confederation of the Rhine in 1813.

Gardes d'Honneur—raised in 1813. Ten squadrons and four regiments, disbanded in 1814. Should not be confused with the *Gardes d'Honneur* belonging to various towns. The *Gardes d'Honneur de la Garde Impériale* were all dressed in Hussar uniforms.

Éclaireurs—raised in 1812, three regiments. 1st attached to the Horse Grenadiers, 2nd to the Dragoons and 3rd (Polish) to the Polish Lancers. (1st and 2nd in Light Dragoons uniforms, 3rd as Polish Lancers.)

Tartares Lithuaniens—raised in 1812 and attached to the Polish Lancers. Incorporated in 1813 into the *Éclaireurs*.

Artillerie à cheval

Artillerie à pied

Train d'Artillerie

Train des Équipages

Sapeurs du Génie

Marins—"Bataillon des Marins de la Garde"

Vétérans,—"Compagnie de Vétérans de la Garde" or "Canonniers-Vétérans"—a Company of *Vétérans Hollandais* raised for service at the Palace in Amsterdam.

Invalids de la Garde Impériale.

After the abdication of Napoleon in April 1814 and the Restoration of Louis XVIII attempts were made to form at least some of the ex-Imperial Guard into a Royal Guard, but this met with little success. The old *Maison du Roi* was however resurrected, including Swiss Guards, *Gardes du Corps*, *Gendarmes* and *Mousquetaires*. When Napoleon returned from exile in March 1815 these short-lived units disappeared.

After Waterloo and the disbandment of the Napoleonic Army the *Maison du Roi* was re-established, and a Royal Order of 1st September 1815 also created a Royal Guard, which was a force of élite field regiments similar to the Imperial Guard, not to be confused with the purely Household Troops.

The Royal Guard consisted of eight three-battalion infantry regiments, two of which were Swiss, and eight cavalry regiments. In addition there were Horse and Foot Artillery, an Artillery Train and a regiment of *Gendarmerie Royale*, also called *Gendarmerie d'Élite*.

The Imperial Guard never had cuirassiers in its Cavalry Arm, but two regiments were included in the new Royal Guard. There were also two regiments of Horse Grenadiers, but only one each of Dragoons, *Chasseurs à cheval*, Lancers, and Hussars.

When Louis XVIII died in 1824, he was succeeded by his brother Charles X, but no important changes were made in the organisation of the Army until 1830 when Louis Philippe appeared on the scene. In accordance with his image as the Citizen King, one of his first moves was to abolish the Royal Guards. He did however attach names connected with his family to certain line units, and on 16th August 1830 the Regiment of Lancers of the disbanded Royal Guard became *Lanciers d'Orléans*.

The next formation of Guards came with the 2nd Empire, and in 1852 a regiment of *Guides* was raised, but it was not until two years later that the last Imperial Guard was created.

On 24th March 1854, a squadron of Household Troops was raised, equipped as cuirassiers, to carry out duties close to the Emperor. This was the *Cent-Gardes* and although part of the Imperial Guard in fact, were always listed separately, and considered senior to the Guard itself.

The Decree of 1st May 1854 established the Imperial Guard. In the mind of Napoleon III at least, this was to be a reincarnation of the Guard raised by his uncle Napoleon I. All Line regiments were asked to select possible candidates for the new Guard regiments, the best soldiers of course being the ones required. At first the Guard was composed of two brigades of infantry, made up of two regiments of Grenadiers, and two of *Voltigeurs*, each with three battalions, with one battalion of *Chasseurs à pied*. There was also a Cavalry Brigade with a six-squadron Cuirassier regiment, and a regiment of *Guides* of the same strength. The inclusion of a cuirassier regiment was a deviation from the custom of the 1st Empire, following the Royal Guard innovation, and unlike previous Guards, Imperial or Royal, there was no Horse Grenadier regiment. Two battalions of Foot *Gendarmerie*, five batteries of Horse Artillery and a company of Engineers completed the Guard at this time. The officers came from Line units and the *Guides* were commanded by Colonel Fleury, who had been so active in trying to give his regiment Guard status in 1852.

The force was soon to be augmented, raising it in fact to an Army Corps in its own right. The Decree of 20th December 1855 shows the addition of a regiment of *Zouaves*, the Infantry of the Guard now forming two complete Divisions of 16 and 17 battalions. The cavalry was substantially increased by the addition of the 2nd Regiment of Cuirassiers, and one regiment each of Dragoons, Lancers, and

14

Chasseurs à cheval, organised into a Cavalry Division of 37 squadrons including a mounted squadron of *Gendarmerie*.

Supporting Arms consisted of 18 batteries of Horse and Foot Artillery, and two companies of Engineers.

Two regiments of *Carabiniers* had continued into the 2nd Empire, as the senior Line cavalry, but in 1865 they ceased to exist, to the great regret of all concerned. At the same time the 2nd Regiment of Cuirassiers of the Guard was absorbed into the 1st Regiment. In view of the many complaints about the disbandment of the *Carabiniers* it was decided to replace the defunct 2nd Cuirassiers by a *Carabinier* Regiment of the Guard. This was put into effect by a decree of November 1865, as a result of which the Imperial Guard included one Cuirassier and one *Carabinier* regiment.

On 25th September 1869 the Foot *Gendarmerie* was disbanded, and in July 1870 the Guard mobilised for War with Prussia. They took the field in two Infantry Divisions, and one Cavalry Division, each with its own Divisional Artillery and Engineers, with additional Reserve Artillery, and the *Train des Équipages* squadron, which operated the supply train. At the end of the campaign the Guard had to be organised into *Régiments de Marche*, or temporary composite units, and the Decree of 28th October 1870, issued by the Government of National Defence, disbanded the Guard altogether. The remaining units, including some now composite, were absorbed into the Line, mostly between February and March 1871.

4. *Imperial Guard Grenadier,*
1804–1814

The Grenadiers and *Chasseurs* of
the Guard were the original Old
Guard, which had been formed from
the Consular Guard.

The uniform had been created
about 1800, Imperial devices being
added in 1804.

The coat was blue of the same
general pattern as that of the Line,
with white breeches and white
gaiters, although black gaiters were
usually worn on the march. Epaulettes, cuffs, and piping were scarlet,
and coat turnbacks were also scarlet
with grenade badges.

Black bearskin caps were everyday
dress for parades and active service.
These had a white cross on a red
patch at the back, but this was later
changed to a grenade. The brass cap-
plate bore the Imperial eagle, and
white cords and red plumes were
worn not only on ceremonial occasions, but in the early days at least,
during active operations. Service or
campaign dress is not a new idea,
but the effect on morale of the Guard
in full regalia was deliberate.

Lapels and equipment were white,
and the black ammunition pouch
was decorated with a brass eagle.
A special short sword was carried in
addition to the bayonet. This latter
was also worn while in walking out
dress, on which occasions a black
bicorn cocked hat replaced the bearskin.

The *Fusiliers-Grenadiers* wore the
same uniform as the Grenadiers,
but they had white epaulettes, and
shakos instead of grenadier caps.

This print is by Charlet, who
himself fought in 1814, and was
possibly the most famous artist of
Imperial Guard subjects.

16

Colour Plate 1. *Imperial Guard Horse Grenadiers, 1804-1814.*
(see page 22)

5. *Imperial Guard Chasseurs à pied, 1804–1814*

The Chasseurs of the Guard shared precedence with the Grenadiers, and wore a very similar uniform, but their piping was white, and their epaulettes were green with red fringes. The coat turnbacks were ornamented with a grenade and a hunting horn in yellow on a white background.

They wore bearskin caps like the Grenadiers, but without a brass plate, and the plume was red over green.

Fusiliers-Chasseurs wore the same uniform, but with a shako instead of a bearskin cap.

This print from a series by Belangé shows a sergeant in walking out dress, and a private in parade order. The sergeant has yellowish knee breeches with white stockings, and wears a dress sword and carries his issue walking-stick. The bicorn hat has a green plume, and is laced with gold. The gold stripe above the cuff is the rank badge, while the chevrons on the left arm are for long service. The private is at the attention position, and has a green woollen sword-knot attached to his short sword. In the case of this figure also, the chevrons on the left arm are long service stripes.

With minor distinctions, and the substitution of shakos for grenadier caps, Foot Guard uniforms were very similar, but the Dutch Guards who were incorporated into the Imperial Guard in 1810 as the 2nd, later 3rd, Grenadiers, wore a white uniform with crimson distinctive colours.

6. *Imperial Guard Tirailleurs-Grenadiers, 1809–1814*

The newer regiments of the Foot Guards wore similar uniforms to the Old Guard, but, with shakos instead of bearskin caps, and they were distinguished by other dress distinctions. The Tirailleurs-Grenadiers of the Young Guard had blue lapels instead of white, and unlike the Grenadiers and Chasseurs had red collars. Short black gaiters slowly replaced the white or long black type as a general rule, although the Grenadiers appear to have clung to the old pattern.

The shako was black, with white chevron-shaped lace on the sides, and red cords. The six regiments were distinguished by their pompon colours. The 1st and 2nd Regiments were red and white, the 1st having the red at the top, the 2nd the reverse. The 3rd was also red and white, but the body of the pompon was red, with a white spot, the 4th was all red, the 5th all white, and the 6th blue with a white spot.

This print by Charlet shows a sergeant of the 1st Regiment in full dress, his gold rank stripe showing above the pointed cuff; a parade plume, also of red and white, is worn above the bi-coloured pompon.

He wears a Legion of Honour, and is obviously an old soldier, possibly promoted from the Old Guard.

The term *Tirailleur* simply means a sharpshooter, or rifleman, but was not normally used as a regimental title, except in the case of modern colonial troops. The pointed cuff on this Guard uniform does however indicate a Light Infantry role.

20

7. *Imperial Guard Grenadier, 1815*

This print by Charlet represents a member of one of the six companies who accompanied the Emperor to Elba, and along with a company of Marines and a squadron of Polish Lancers shared his exile.

During the early days the Guard wore full dress on most occasions, but blue trousers had replaced the breeches and gaiters by this time, and the bearskin caps were usually without cords. A notable point about the Guards was that they never received the 1812 pattern short coatee, but from the beginning to the end wore the old long-tailed coat, which exposed the waistcoat in front.

The Elba Battalion, as it was called, returned with Napoleon, and formed part of the 1st Grenadiers at Waterloo, four out of five of which were holders of the Legion of Honour.

Uniforms were not in a good state at the last battle, and some of the Guard regiments were reduced to wearing Line uniforms, and one battalion was dressed in National Guard clothing. Bearskin caps were in very short supply, and even shakos were not available in sufficient quantity.

The 1st Grenadiers, however, appear to have been reasonably well turned out, although contrary to popular legend, and the imagination of romantic modern artists the Guard at Waterloo were not the spectacular sight of former years.

Too much is perhaps based on Waterloo in modern visions of the Napoleonic Army, where they probably were at their worst as far as appearance was concerned.

21

Colour Plate **1** (Page 17).
Imperial Guard Horse Grenadiers, 1804–1814

The senior cavalry regiment of the Guard, nicknamed *"gros talons"* (big heels), they were derived from the mounted grenadiers of the Consular Guard. The uniform was very similar to the Foot Guards, but with several distinctive features. The bearskin caps had no brass plate, and the cap cords, epaulettes, and the aiguilettes worn on the right shoulder, were of a shade of orange and called *"aurore"*. Long, stiff boots were worn in full dress, but when on campaign a second pair of soft leather were used.

The shabraque was blue, with orange edging, a crown being displayed at each corner, but some contemporary evidence indicates that a grenade was sometimes used; the same doubts arise over the number of flaps on the holster covers (*chaperons*) as, although three was normal, some old prints show two.

The Officers' own lace and that on their horse furniture, was gold. They also had gold epaulettes, only senior officers having fringes on both; troopers had no fringes at all.

The uniforms of this regiment were particularly fine, the products of the foremost tailors, hatters and bootmakers in Paris. The horses were superb, being carefully selected blacks of about 15 hands. It is not surprising that in a period of four years nearly twenty million francs were spent on the clothing of the Imperial Guard alone.

This is the regiment which, disdainful of the rabble around them, declined to take part in the Waterloo rout, and according to British reports left the field at an organised walk march in their own good time.

1. (Frontispiece). *Imperial Guard Chasseurs à cheval, 1804–1815*

This regiment was formed in July 1804 from the *Chasseurs* and *Guides* of the Consular Guard. Unlike the *Chasseurs à cheval* of the Line who wore full hussar costume of particularly fine quality, including a green dolman and a fur-trimmed scarlet pelisse. Fine Hungarian boots were worn with yellow doeskin breeches for parades, and equally good quality green Hungarian breeches on service. The fur cap had a scarlet top and flap (*flamme*) on the right side, with a green and red plume on the left.

Trumpeters were particularly spectacular, with sky-blue dolmans, red pelisses and white caps, this regiment being among the most expensively dressed in the whole army.

The *Chasseurs à cheval* of the Guard had five squadrons of 250 men in 1811, and nine squadrons in 1813. At Waterloo, where they carried out their traditional task of acting as immediate escort to the Emperor, they consisted of four squadrons.

In undress uniform they wore a green overcoat (*surtout*), and it was this that Napoleon normally wore alternately with the blue coat of the Foot Guards, when in military costume.

This uniform was worn throughout the period of the Empire, but later breeches were worn only on parades, and as in other sections of the cavalry, buttoned overalls, first green and then grey, were worn on active service.

This drawing by Victor Adam shows an officer in full dress.

22

8. *Imperial Guard Gendarmes d'Élite, 1804*

The Legion of Élite Gendarmes raised in 1804 consisted of horse and foot contingents, although the mounted squadrons are perhaps better known. They had a uniform not unlike the Horse Grenadiers of the Guard, but with red lapels, cuffs and coat turnbacks, their white aiguillettes being worn on the left shoulder. Breeches were yellowish buckskin, worn with high black boots. Their bearskin caps had white metal chin-scales, a white grenade on a red patch on the top rear; a leather peak was also a characteristic feature.

The foot companies had a very similar uniform, but with red epaulettes, gaiters replacing the leather riding boots.

Trumpeters of the horse squadrons, and drummers of the foot companies wore scarlet coats.

The kettle drum was considered a Royal instrument in France, coming to them from the Turks via Hungary, and its use was at this time, officially at least, the privilege of Guard units. Captured drums are often mentioned in old battle reports and were given similar status to flags. Kettle-drums were very valuable objects, the drummers being provided with an escort, but a pretence was later made that infantry side-drums were of similar status as spoils of victory, which was not the case at all.

This fine engraving, published in 1804 by Jean of Paris, shows the mounted drummer wearing the same dress as trumpeters with the cocked hat worn in full dress. This specimen is in the original form, not in the overpainted state sometimes found.

9. *Imperial Guard Dragoons, 1806–1814*

The Dragoons of the Guard, known from 1807 as the Empress's Dragoons, wore a jacket similar to the Horse Grenadiers, with orange aiguillettes, but in dragoon green. The piping was scarlet, and the epaulettes without fringes were orange. The white breeches and boots were of the same pattern as the Grenadiers. Helmets were of the heavy cavalry pattern made of brass, with a panther skin turban, black *houpette* or front tuft, and the side plume, worn on parade, was red. Officers, as shown on this print by Victor Adam, had gold epaulettes, aiguillettes and horse furniture decoration. The helmets of the commissioned ranks were particularly fine, being gilded, with real animal skin turbans, while in later years at least, those of the men appear to have been artificial.

The sword shown here is the officer's pattern with gilded hilt and fittings; the grenade device was also worn on the coat turnbacks.

When the regiment was raised 12 men, each with a minimum of ten years' service, were selected from each Line dragoon regiment, and a system of promotion to the Guard from the Line continued throughout the period of the Empire.

The trumpeters looked superb in white uniforms with sky-blue lapels, epaulettes and cuffs, and gold lace. Their helmets had blue plumes, and white manes instead of the usual black.

10. *Imperial Guard Lancers,*
1809–1814

This print shows the 1st Light Horse Lancers of the Guard in their distinctive Polish uniform. This regiment, recruited from Poles in 1807, was armed with lances in 1809, and was among the most distinguished units of the Guard. The uniform jacket (*Kurtka*) was blue with crimson lapels, and the trousers were crimson with double blue stripes. Epaulettes and aiguillettes were white. The most characteristic feature was the head-dress, normally known by its Polish name, *Czapska*, a style later to be copied by the other nations of the world for troops armed with the lance.

The 2nd Regiment also wore Polish uniform, but was Dutch in origin, the men being Dutch and French. This regiment wore red jackets, with yellow epaulettes and aiguillettes, and was as well known as "The Red Lancers"

The 3rd Regiment, raised in 1812

lasted only a few months, and was dressed exactly like the 1st but with gold lace instead of silver.

At Waterloo the Lancers of the Guard were represented by what was nominally four squadrons of the 2nd *Lanciers Rouges*, as far as uniform was concerned, but the men came from the recently formed Royal Guard and from other units. In addition to these, one squadron consisted of the Elba detachment of Poles, still dressed in the blue of the 1st Regiment. Reports indicate that only the front rank of each squadron were armed with lances at Waterloo.

11. *Imperial Guard Scout, 1813*

The three regiments of *Éclaireurs* were raised in 1813, and are interesting units of the Guard. They were counted as one corps, being numbered 1st, 2nd, and 3rd *Éclaireurs*, but each regiment had its own distinctive uniforms.

The 1st Regiment was divided into Old Guard and Young Guard sections, the Old Guard being dressed in hussar uniform with green dolman and pelisse, and black shako, while the Young Guard had a green coatee with no pelisse. Red Hungarian breeches were worn at first, but these were later changed to grey buttoned overalls.

This print shows the 2nd Regiment, in a green chasseur coatee and buttoned overalls with the crimson stripe which was their distinctive colour. An eagle was placed on the shabraque corner in all three regiments. The shako is of particular interest as it is of the cylindrical type which was coming into use at this time. It was cheaper and easier to manufacture than the normal pattern, and the style lasted into the Restoration period. This one was crimson the same as the distinctive colours on the uniform collar and cuffs. Lances appear to have been carried, but there is no mention of them in the original orders for the 1st and 2nd Regiments, who were attached to the Horse Grenadiers and the Dragoons of the Guard.

The 3rd *Éclaireurs*, composed of Poles, were attached to the 1st Lancers of the Guard, and wore virtually the same Polish uniform, although they do not appear ever to have had any other leg-wear than grey buttoned overalls.

12. *Cent-Gardes-Suisses, 1814*

The old *Maison du Roi* had in
addition to the French Guards in
blue and the Swiss Guards in scarlet,
a special company of Swiss which
ranked with the immediate Royal
body-guards.

This unit wore the royal livery,
with red collars and gold lace. In
the palace they wore gold laced
cocked hats with Swiss national
costume, but in service dress they
wore bearskin caps and French
Guard uniforms.

During the very brief Restoration
period before Waterloo, they were
re-formed with the other household
troops. Their uniform colours were
the same, but were brought up to
date—undoubtedly under Napoleonic
influence.

This 1815 print, after Martinet,
shows a drummer of the *Cent-
Suisse* between the time of the abdication of Napoleon in 1814, and
March 1815. Because of the time
required to produce the new Royal
uniforms this could only have been
worn for a few months, because the
unit was not re-formed at the Second
Restoration after Waterloo.

The plate on the bearskin cap
bears the Royal arms and the blue
coat is richly adorned with gold,
including the traditional drummer's
arm chevrons.

The breeches of the company
itself were blue, or white for full
dress, but in the case of this drummer
they were red. A white protective
apron was worn to minimise wear
from the movement of the drum.

28

13. *Royal Guards, 1815*

The new Royal Guard infantry raised by Louis XVIII were dressed in blue jackets, white breeches and black gaiters. The jacket was now the short, straight-fronted type, but instead of lapels it had nine white metal buttons with nine bars of white lace (*brandebourgs*). Bearskin caps were worn by the grenadier companies, the others having shakos.

Each of the six regiments was distinguished by the colour of jacket turnbacks and cuffs, collars were blue in all cases, and grenades, bugle-horns, and fleur de lys on the turnbacks identified the different companies.

Grenadiers wore red epaulettes, *voltigeurs* orange, centre companies white, and *chasseurs* green.

Two Swiss regiments were included in the Foot Guards, known as the 1st and 2nd Swiss, but also 7th and 8th Foot Guards. They wore scarlet uniforms, the two regiments displaying variations of blue on cuffs, collar, etc.

The *Maison du Roi*, the immediate Household units, are represented in this contemporary print by the *Garde du Corps du Roi*. All its companies wore the same uniform with scarlet collar and on the other positions for the normal distinctive colours, but they were identified by the colour of the squares on the pouch belt, a very unusual method. There were four companies at first, with white, green, blue, and yellow belts, a fifth added later had scarlet.

Lace and buttons were silver, and the special helmet was blackened with white metal, or silvered decoration. A laced cocked hat was also worn.

29

14. *Royal Guard, 1816*

The cavalry of the Royal Guard wore uniforms which were strongly reminiscent of their Imperial predecessors, and this illustration, which is a section of an important print published in 1816, shows that they were just as picturesque.

The small figure in the background represents the Artillery Train in a grey uniform and black helmet with fur crest, a modified resurrection of the 1792 type, but even more like the British "Tarleton".

The Horse Grenadier (left) still had the characteristics of the Napoleonic regiment, but the long-tailed blue coat had seven *brandebourgs* on the chest, and epaulettes, aiguilettes, and bearskin cords were white. The two regiments existing at this period were identified by the white plume of the 1st, or the red and white plume and red collar and cuffs of the 2nd.

There were no cuirassiers in the Imperial Guard but two regiments were included in the King's Guard (centre). Both wore red piped blue jackets with white epaulettes, a sun burst with the Arms of France and Navarre being displayed on the steel cuirass. Helmets were the same as the type introduced in 1802, but the horsehair mane and front plume were replaced by a fur crest or caterpillar (*Chenille*). Both had white plumes, but the 2nd Regiment had a red ball at the base. In 1826 a new helmet without the skin turban was issued, but the 2nd Regiment did not receive theirs until the following year. Helmets were supposed to last ten years, so they were due for replacement in any case.

30

Continued

The single regiment of dragoons (right) wore the traditional green in the form of a short coatee with rose coloured lapels. The helmet was brass with a tiger skin turban and had the fur crest which was now the Royalist fashion.

15. *Royal Guard Horse Artillery, 1816*

This engraving, from an important series published in 1816, shows the uniform of the Horse Artillery as they were in that year.

The uniform is blue with scarlet piping, epaulettes and cords. The regulations state that Hungarian breeches were worn, but blue overalls, with a double scarlet stripe, and reinforced with leather were used, at least on service. It appears that a shako covered with fur was worn at first, but a proper Hussar kolback with a scarlet bag was issued in December 1815. This had a white plume with a scarlet base, and the white cockade was displayed at the base of the plume.

The pointed shabraque was blue with scarlet edging, a crown, and the Royal Cypher of intertwined Ls was embroïdered at the corners. The sword, in a steel scabbard, was the brass hilted 1816 light cavalry pattern.

The foot artillery had a very similar uniform, worn with a black shako.

31

16. *Royal Guard Hussar, 1816*

There had been no hussars in the Imperial Guard although the *Chasseurs à cheval* of the Guard were sometimes nicknamed "Hussars of the Guard" because of their pelisses and general appearance.

The one hussar regiment of the new Royal Guard was a fine corps dressed according to the accepted Hungarian traditions with royal blue dolmans and pelisses with scarlet collars and cuffs. Breeches were crimson, loopings and all piping were white. Pelisses were edged with black fur, and the sabretache and valise were decorated with a shield bearing the royal arms and with a fleur-de-lys respectively.

At first this regiment was given a shako covered with black felt, but very shortly after, this was replaced by a black fur cap (*kolback*) with a red top and bag; a tall white plume with a red base being fitted in full dress.

The shabraque was the same shade of blue as the uniform, with red and white edging. As in the case of all guard cavalry, intertwined Ls surmounted by a crown were placed at the corners.

This print, from a drawing by Carle Vernet, is interesting as it clearly shows the H for Hussars, with a crown above, branded on the horse's thigh.

The 1816 model light cavalry sword with three bar hilt was not carried by this regiment, who continued to use the hussar pattern of the Empire.

17. *Royal Guard Infantry, 1823*

The infantry of the Royal Guard after 1822 wore the same uniform as that ordered for the Line, but with nine bars of lace or *brandebourgs* sewn on the chest of the single-breasted jacket. Grenadiers had bearskin caps, and all six French regiments had an overcoat of a darker blue than the grey-blue pattern issued to the Line. The 1st, 2nd and 3rd Regiments had crimson, rose and yellow cuffs, and jacket turnbacks; the 4th, 5th and 6th had the same distinctive colours but in their case the cuffs themselves were the same colour as the jacket, the colour being shown on the cuff patch.

Breeches and gaiters were now replaced by white trousers in summer, and by blue in winter like the Infantry of the Line.

The two Swiss regiments, the 7th and 8th, retained their scarlet in the new style, and whereas they previously had been distinguished by blue lapels, they now had single-breasted jackets with bars of lace like the six French regiments.

Epaulettes were white in all cases, and heavy white cords adorned the shakos of the fusiliers and the bearskin caps of the grenadiers.

This print published at the time shows a fusilier of the Swiss Royal Guard.

Although many foreign troops served the French monarchs, including Scots and Irish from a very early period, it was the Swiss who became most identified with the French Army, and it was mainly Swiss officers and N.C.O.s who organised and trained the Foreign Legion when first raised in 1831.

33

18. *Royal Guard Lancers, 1823*

When the new Royal Guard was formed in 1815 one lancer regiment was included, which had a lineage to the 2nd Lancers of the Imperial Guard. In 1830 most of its personnel formed the *Lanciers d'Orléans*, being designated the 6th Orléans Lancers in 1831. This regiment was transformed into the 18th Dragoons in 1871. However, another line of descent is claimed in the regimental histories, as the Royal Guard Lancers, which are the subject of this print, were also the forerunners of the Lancers of the Imperial Guard of the Second Empire, which in August were absorbed into the 20th Dragoons after a brief period of fusion, from April 1871, with the 6th Lancers.

When enjoying their lancer roles all these units wore Polish dress, those of the Royal Guard, one of whose officers is shown here, had green jackets with a crimson plastron and white epaulettes and aiguillettes. Trousers were originally green with a double white stripe, but by 1823, when this print was published, these had been changed to crimson. The *czapska* was crimson with black lace in 1816, but in 1832 it was white.

Officers' cords and epaulettes were silver instead of white and a crowned lily device decorated the corners of the shabraque.

Lances were of the Polish type, nine feet long with pennons measuring 62cm by 44cm (about 24in by 17in). In fact the lances brought to France by Napoleon's Poles were standard all over the world for many years.

34

Colour Plate 2. *Colour-Bearer, 1830.*
(see page 58)

19. *Royal Guard Mounted Bandsman, 1825*

Since an artillery train had been fully incorporated into the army structure they had worn grey uniforms, although there is always some doubt as to how much blue has in fact been in the *gris de fer* of the regulations. The train of the Royal Guard at first wore a version of the British "Tarleton" helmet, but by 1825 this had been replaced by a more French type with a curved crest like the *carabiniers*. This charming contemporary lithograph shows a bandsman of the Artillery Train of the Royal Guard of this period, the cypher of Charles X being clearly shown on the shabraque.

The crest of the black leather helmet is red, this being normal for trumpeters and bandsmen; the grey horse was usual for such members of a mounted unit. The uniform was blue with silver lace, red epaulettes and red trouser stripe. It will be noticed that the trombone bell points to the rear.

Cavalry bands of the First Empire had 16 trumpeters, six horns and three trombones, although Napoleon abolished them for a time as being a waste of men and horses. However by 1845 mounted bands normally consisted of 36 players, the infantry having 54.

At the time of the Second Empire the Imperial Guard had 55 players, and the cavalry 35, although the cavalry musicians were all returned to normal duty again in 1867.

Despite the insecure position of actual cavalry bands, French mounted units always maintained *fanfares*. These were originally composed of regimental trumpeters, who had developed a characteristic and rousing technique of their own.

20. *Cent-Gardes, 1854–1870*

The squadron of *Cent-Gardes* were the Imperial equivalent to the *Maison du Roi* troops of the kings of France, and carried out guard duties within the palaces, and acted as close escort to the Emperor.

They took precedence over all troops in France, including the Imperial Guard, and were dressed in specially fine uniforms.

For mounted duty they wore steel cuirasses and sky-blue tunics with purple collars, cuffs and piping; epaulettes were scarlet with gold fringes, and white buckskin breeches were worn with fine long boots.

The helmet was white metal without a turban, but with a triangular brass plate bearing the letter N. The mane flowing from a brass crest was white, as was the front tuft.

On dismounted duty a cuirass made of buff cloth with the Imperial Arms embroidered on front replaced the metal one, and a walking-out

dress with purple trousers and a cocked hat was peculiar to this élite corps. The 1860 regulations refer to *Garance* (madder red) trousers, and scarlet collars, but the first descriptions say purple.

Trumpeters wore red coats with gold lace.

An unusual feature was the special *Cent-Garde fusil-lance*, which was an early experiment in small-calibre weapons, and one which tried out the idea of cavalry swords being used to turn rifles, or carbines, into lances.

This unit was quite small, as its title indicates, consisting of 11 officers and 137 N.C.O.s and men. It is interesting to note that long before modern interest in uniforms was aroused few real examples of the uniform of this corps existed, and reproductions were being made for sale as genuine. This is mentioned in the history of the regiment by Albert Verly, son of the commanding officer, published in 1894.

21. *Imperial Guard Grenadiers, 1854–1860*

The Grenadiers of Louis Napoleon's Imperial Guard were, visually at least, a reincarnation of the legendary soldiers of the First Empire, with the inevitable differences made necessary in costume fashion in general by the passage of time.

Although the modern French soldier created by Louis Philippe continued in the new Empire, the Guard returned to the old long-tailed coat with white lapels for full dress, although these lapels were now of the plastron shape already worn by certain mounted units. The now universal red trousers were also a departure from the historical uniform of Imperial Guards. The coat was blue with red collar and epaulettes; cuffs were also red with white cuff patches.

A bearskin cap of true Napoleonic grandeur was worn, complete with a brass plate, or frontlet, bearing the Imperial eagle, which device with the words *Garde Impériale* was also inscribed on the brass buttons of the coat.

In undress (*petite tenue*) a felt cocked hat with a scarlet plume was worn.

This lithograph by de Moraine, published when the corps was formed, shows back and front views of the new uniform in all its splendour.

The small pouch attached to the shoulder belt for the cartridge box was the container for percussion caps for the musket.

39

22. *Imperial Guard Voltigeurs, 1854–1860*

The two original infantry units of the old Imperial Guard were Grenadiers and *Chasseurs*, and the same ideas motivated the creation of their Second Empire successors.

The grenadier and light companies of French infantry regiments were both classed as *élite* companies, so the new Infantry of the Guard were in fact whole regiments bearing the titles of what were already the *élite* categories of the ordinary infantry.

The dress of the *Voltigeurs* was very similar to the Grenadiers, collars and coat turnbacks were however yellow, and instead of the so-called "French" cuff, pointed "Polish" cuffs in yellow pipe conformed to Light Infantry usage.

The epaulettes were red, but the shoulder straps had yellow piping. Trousers were described as blue with a yellow stripe in the original orders, but these were changed to red with a blue stripe.

Shakos had heavy white cords, worn in full dress with yellow and white plumes. In undress, or walking-out order, the white plastrons were replaced by blue lapels, and cocked hats were worn instead of shakos.

Hunting horns were much in evidence on ammunition pouches and turnbacks, but in general equipment was the same as the Grenadiers.

During the period of formation the various Guard units had depots in or near Paris; the 1st *Voltigeurs* were at St. Denis, the 2nd at Versailles, and it was at these depots that the selected men were organised and fitted for their new uniforms before being inspected by the Emperor.

40

23. *Imperial Guard Chasseurs à pied 1854–1860*

The *Chasseurs à pied* as a major infantry corps had to be represented in the Guard, and 20 First Class privates from each Line *Chasseur* battalion were called for to act as a nucleus. The most experienced officers were also invited to join the new Imperial unit. Uniform was in accordance with the accepted principles but with important differences. In 1860 the ordinary infantry and *chasseurs* of the Line replaced their long tunics for the short *habit tunique*, but the *Chasseurs* of the Guard had worn this for some time before. They also wore the voluminous breeches generally adopted in 1860. Illustrations sometimes give the impression that bare calves appear above the gaiters, but these were brown leather leggings called *jambières*.

The uniform was blue with green epaulettes, the breeches were grey, with a tendency to blue, and the piping was yellow.

The shako was covered with blue cloth and chevron-shaped yellow lace decorated the sides—a relic of the 1st Empire to indicate *élite* troops. The falling plume was officially black, but appears to have been dark green in some actual specimens. Although a hunting horn was the universal badge of *Chasseurs* and Light Infantry, an eagle badge was worn on the belt buckle, this again being the indication of an *élite* formation. Officers wore the old long tunic. A "fore and aft" *bonnet de police* was used in undress.

In 1846 all *chasseurs* were issued with *Minié* rifles, and had brass-hilted sabre bayonets instead of the normal socket type.

In 1860 yellow hussar type loopings were added to the breast of the tunic.

At the siege of Sebastopol this regiment carried out a ferocious attack on the redoubts during which the Colonel, four officers and 99 men were killed on or inside the fortifications.

41

24. *Imperial Guard Zouaves, 1855–1870*

The regiments of *Zouaves* raised by Louis Philippe had distinguished themselves continually since their creation in 1830, and in addition to the two extra regiments raised in 1852, their prowess was rewarded by inclusion in the Guard in 1855.

Although the men were French, the dress was North African, the different Line regiments being distinguished by the colour of the false pockets on the jacket, red for the 1st, white for the 2nd, and yellow for the 3rd.

The Decree raising the *Zouaves* of the Guard established two battalions of seven companies each, forming part of the 1st Brigade on the left of the 2nd Grenadiers. Officers came from the *Chasseurs à pied*, Algerian *Tirailleurs*, and European African Light Infantry; other ranks were selected from the *Chasseurs* and *Zouaves* of the Line.

The Uniform was of the complete *Zouave* style; blue jacket and waistcoat with yellow lace, red cuffs with light infantry pointed piping in yellow, red cap (*chéchia*) with yellow tassel surrounded by a white turban.

The red trousers were of Arab design, and leather *jambières* were worn with white gaiters.

These troops should not be confused with native African units, and were, despite their appearance, French Light Infantry with a similar role to the *Chasseurs à pied*.

This regiment was formed in the Crimea, and also fought at Solferino and Magenta. After 1870 it was absorbed into the new 4th Zouaves of the Line.

25. *Imperial Guard Foot-Guards, 1860–1870*

While the Infantry of the Line wore their long tunics, the Grenadiers and *Voltigeurs* of the Imperial Guard had reverted to the obsolete tailed coat for full dress. However in 1860 the guard adopted tunics, while the Line began to wear the new very short *habit-tunique.*

The new guard tunic was dark blue single-breasted with nine bars, or *brandebourgs*, made of wool thread, white for the grenadiers, and yellow for the *Voltigeurs*. Grenadiers' collars and epaulettes were scarlet, and they wore the traditional bearskin cap, while *voltigeurs* had yellow collars and their red epaulettes were laced with yellow piping. The 1860 pattern all-leather shako was issued to *Voltigeurs*, with an eagle plate and red and yellow plume. When the full plume was not worn, a small yellow pompon replaced it. Although the new guard uniform was completely changed in October 1860, the new design had been approved earlier, and in April 1860 the old white cross belts had been changed for the equipment used by the Line.

This uniform was worn in 1870, but normally with a *bonnet de police*, and with the trousers inside the gaiters, at least after the first weeks of the war.

After 1870 these guard regiments were fused with the Line of the new army—1st Grenadiers with 94th, 1st *Voltigeurs* with 96th, others with the 84th, 98th, and 100th, and the remaining odd companies with the 28th *Régiment de Marche*, later the 128th.

26. *Imperial Guard Guides,*
1854–1870

On 23rd October 1852 Colonel
Fleury, impatient to command an
élite cavalry corps, succeeded in
obtaining authority to raise a regiment of Guides for duty with the
new Emperor. These were formed
from two squadrons of reliable
mounted Guards which existed in
1851, augmented by various detach-
ments from dragoons, lancers, and
chasseurs d'Afrique, making up a
regiment of six squadrons. Fleury's
success in creating a unit fine in the
quality of both its men and its horses,
did much to encourage the idea of a
new Imperial Guard, despite the
doubts of the General Staff. When
the Guard was formed, the regiment
was designated *Guides de la Garde
Impériale* on 1st May 1854, under

the command of Colonel Fleury.

They wore a hussar uniform with
a green dolman lavishly decorated
with 18 loops of a particular colour
of golden yellow, which was used
for all piping, aiguillettes etc. Collar
and cuffs were red and breeches
were red with a double gold stripe.
A black fur cap with a black and
white plume was worn in full dress,
a very smart red and green *bonnet de
police* in undress.

Pelisses are not mentioned in the
first dress descriptions but a green
one was worn later, and always by
officers in court dress.

During the reorganisation of the
cavalry in 1871 the 9th Hussars
were formed from the Guides and
the 9th Light Cavalry *de Marche*,
which had been raised in January
1871.

27. *Imperial Guard Cuirassiers, 1854*

The six-squadron regiment of cuirassiers included in the Guard of Napoleon III was one deviation from his uncle's rules, and continued an idea started by the restored monarchy in 1815.

The 1st Regiment wore a long dark blue tunic, not the usual cavalry jacket. It was worn with the skirts turned back and had scarlet distinctives, white epaulettes and aiguillettes. White breeches with high boots were worn in full dress, but red trousers on some dismounted duties and for walking out.

The helmet was steel without a turban and was similar to the *Cent-Gardes* model, but with a black mane.

The 2nd Regiment, created in 1855, had the same design of uniform but the tunic was sky-blue, and they had sky-blue piping on their red trousers, whereas the 1st Regiment had dark blue piping.

The cuirass was steel, all belts were white, and an eagle badge was displayed on the cartridge box or pouch.

A *bonnet de police* with scarlet piping was worn in undress.

When the 2nd Regiment was absorbed into the 1st in 1865 the sky-blue uniforms disappeared, and the one remaining regiment wore dark blue.

The *Cent-Garde* trumpeters had scarlet coats with *brandebourgs* on the breast; those of the Cuirassiers of the Guard were very much the same but in blue. When the Guard ceased to exist this regiment was absorbed into the 12th Cuirassiers of the line in 1871.

28. *Imperial Guard Dragoons, 1856*

Dragoons were added during the general augmentation of the Imperial Guard, taking upon themselves the old title of *Dragons de l'Impératrice* in 1857 so proudly claimed by their First Empire predecessors, the Empress now of course being the beautiful Eugénie. The men were selected from candidates among the best looking and most effective soldiers of the Dragoons of the Line.

The uniform was green, with white lapels of plastron shape for full dress, although these were not worn un undress uniform. Collars were red, and a double green stripe adorned the red breeches, which had leather false boots in the now prevailing fashion for mounted duty.

Helmets were brass with black horsehair manes, but as was the case in other Guard helmets, no skin turban was fitted as in Line versions.

Shabraques were green with white and red edging, adorned with a crowned N. Aiguillettes and epaulettes were white, and white gloves rather than gauntlets were worn in full dress.

The remarkably inconvenient method of carrying the firearm in a butt-down position over the right leg was still a dragoon characteristic.

At this period a curved sword was carried instead of the more normal straight bladed heavy cavalry model.

In 1870 they continued as a regiment called *Régiment de Dragons de l'Ex-Garde*, a most unusual distinction, but from 1871 their lineage is taken over by the 13th Dragoons.

Infantry of the Line

In 1789 there were 101 regiments of infantry bearing Royal or territorial titles, but an Order by the National Assembly dated 1st January 1791 replaced all titles by plain numbers. In July of the same year the foreign regiments of the French Service were assimilated into the new system, and by 1792 had lost their foreign character.

As long as Louis XVI was alive these numbered regiments were part of an army owing theoretical allegiance to the King as well as the National Assembly, but the Decrees of 21st February and 12th August 1793 created a Republican Army and abolished the title of regiment altogether.

The Infantry of the Line was now composed of 198 demi-brigades, consisting of three battalions, each having one old regular battalion and two of the new volunteers. This organisation continued· until the Consular Order of 24th September 1803 re-established numbered regiments. In 1793 some light infantry units had been transformed into *demi-brigades légères* but the 1803 Order created 27 new Regiments of Light Infantry. The infantry regiments of the 1st Empire varied in quantity and strength, but the raising of 44 new regiments in the five years up to 1813 increased the total from 112 to 156. A Napoleonic regiment was normally made up of two or three battalions, each usually consisting of about six companies, and after 13th September 1805, when light companies were added to line units, a battalion had one grenadier, four to six fusilier, and one light or *Voltigeur* company. In the French Army Fusiliers were not a special type of unit, but simply the centre companies, as opposed to the élite or flank companies of *grenadiers* or *voltigeurs*.

The Regiments of Light Infantry of Napoleon's Army varied from 31 to 37, and were separate from the ordinary infantry. They too had their flank companies, in this case the grenadiers were called *Carabiniers*, and it is perhaps surprising that they, like the ordinary infantry, had *Voltigeur* companies.

After the defeat of 1814 and Napoleon's expulsion to Elba, the restored Royalist régime had plans for a re-organisation of the infantry into 100 regiments, including 15 of Light Infantry. There was, however, no time to put this into operation before the return of the Emperor, and the subsequent Waterloo campaign.

After Waterloo, and the second Restoration of Louis XVIII steps were taken to remove all traces of the Revolution and Empire and a vital step in this direction was the total disbandment of the Army. This was carried out in accordance with a Royal Order in August 1815. The infantry regiments once again disappeared, to be replaced by 87 Departmental Legions, identified not by numbers, but by the name of the department, or region, in which they were raised. These legions had three battalions at first, but a fourth was added in 1819. The Regiments of Light Infantry had been abolished, but one battalion of the Legions was classed as *Chasseurs à pied*, which was simply a return to an old title for a similar role.

The Departmental Legions existed until an Order of October 23rd 1820 restored numbered regiments. This Order created 60 Line Infantry Regiments and 20 Regiments of Light Infantry. On 2nd February 1823 the 61st, 62nd, 63rd and 64th Regiments were raised, all having a strength of three battalions.

The accession of Charles X in 1824 brought no changes in organisation, but during the reign of Louis Philippe from 1830 to 1848 new regiments were raised, and the basis of the French Army as it was to exist for many years was established.

The infantry was the backbone of the Army of Africa, and in addition to the 49 Line and 13 Light regiments which fought in Algeria between 1831 and 1848 other famous units were raised in this period. The *Zouaves* in 1830, the Foreign Legion in 1831, *Infanterie Légère d'Afrique* in 1832, and a completely new corps of riflemen, first called *Tirailleurs de Vincennes* when they were created in 1838. The title was changed to *Chasseurs d'Orléans* in 1842, the corps being increased in strength to 10 battalions.

On 8th September 1841 an important Order laid out the organisation of the infantry, and the 1846 *Annuaire Militaire* lists the following:

100 Regiments	75 regiments	Infantry of the Line
	25 regiments	Light Infantry
	10 battalions	*Chasseurs d'Orléans*
	1 regiment	*Zouaves*
	3 battalions	*Infanterie Légère d'Afrique*
	8 companies	*Fusiliers de Discipline*
	4 companies	*Pionniers de Discipline*
	2 regiments	Foreign Legion
	3 battalions	*Tirailleurs Indigènes*
	10 companies	Veterans.

Infantry regiments had three battalions each, and the battalions of *Chasseurs d'Orléans* had eight companies. In 1848 the reign of Louis Philippe came to an end, but during the period of the second Republic infantry organisation was unchanged, except for the removal of Orléans titles, the *Chasseurs d'Orléans* becoming *Chasseurs à pied*. The troops of this famous corps should not be confused with any units, or sub-divisions, with the same title at earlier periods. The battalions of *Chasseurs à pied* which have borne the title from 1848 to modern times have a continuous lineage only to the Corps raised in 1838 as *Tirailleurs de Vincennes*.

In 1852 the Second Empire reintroduced Imperial insignia, but the Order of 1841 was still officially the basis for the organisation of the infantry and only one major change occurred. This was the final abolition of Regiments of Light Infantry. On 24th October 1854 these units were absorbed into the ordinary infantry, receiving the numbers 76–100 of the Line. All the functions of light troops were completely taken over by the *Chasseurs à pied*, whose strength was brought up to 20 battalions. Two new regiments of *Zouaves* were raised in 1852, and the North African Native Riflemen were increased to three full regiments as *Tirailleurs Algériens* in 1855.

Although the Foreign Legion had two regiments at most times, it had only one between 1862 and 1875, and in 1863 the *Companies de Discipline* had been reduced to seven in all. The Paris Fire Brigade, as part of the Army, was listed under Infantry and ranked after the *Zouaves*, with the title *Bataillon de Sapeurs-Pompiers de la Ville de Paris* as a unit of ten companies.

The internal regimental organisation was unchanged, i.e. three battalions of eight companies, including grenadiers and *Voltigeurs*. This was however altered on 22nd January 1868, when the flank companies were abolished in all regiments.

After the War of 1870 the Infanry of the Line was established at 144 regiments, and 30 battalions of *Chasseurs à pied*.

Many other infantry formations fought under the French flag, including numerous Foreign and Special Corps, and changes of identity and status in time of War, or under different régimes, can cause confusion. Similar titles for totally different units and formations, at various periods, must also be taken into consideration, such as the organisation of *Gendarmerie* into Departmental Legions, which has nothing to do with the 1815 Infantry system.

Regimental continuity in the British sense does not exist in the French Army, and frequent disbandments and alterations of organisation by changing régimes appear to make claims for a regimental lineage very tenuous indeed. However, it is very important indeed to realise that the Order of September 1841 established a basic infantry organisation, still quoted as such in official publications dealing with the new Army of the 1870s, which in turn developed into the one that took the field in 1914.

29. *Infantry, 1790*

The infantry uniforms introduced by the regulations of October 1786 were to establish the basic style which would continue until the last years of the Empire.

All Line regiments wore white coats, breeches and waistcoats, regimental distinctive colours being shown on collars, lapels, cuffs, and in some cases, on the coat turnbacks.

The normal headdress was a cocked hat with coloured plumes to identify the various companies, the ornaments on the turnbacks of the coat also distinguishing grenadier, centre, and light companies.

Officers' uniforms were similar to those of the men, but in finer material with epaulettes, and with metal gorgets worn at the neck.

In 1755 bearskin caps made their first appearance in the French Army, and in 1767 they were officially sanctioned for grenadiers. An instruction of 1775 confirmed their use, fixing the period of wear at ten years, but in 1776 they were abolished. This last order was not generally obeyed, and in 1789 a supplement to the 1786 regulations restored them again.

This print shows a grenadier of the *Régiment de Flandre*, which became the 19th Regiment in 1791. The lapels, collar and cuffs were violet, and although black gaiters are shown here, white were worn in full dress.

30. *Infantry, 1795*

For some time the soldiers of the Revolution wore a confused variety of uniforms basically those of the Royalist army.

In April 1791 the tricolour cockade was introduced and at the same time a leather helmet, similar to the "Tarleton" of British light dragoons, was ordered for all infantry. These were only worn for two years however, and not all units were issued with them.

When regiments were abolished in 1793 the blue uniform, previously worn by the National Guard, and already issued to some Line units, was made standard for the demibrigades and began to replace the motley pieces of clothing which had passed for uniform.

This print shows the regulation uniform which by the time of the Consulate had been issued to all infantry. White breeches and black gaiters were an acceptance of the military dress conventions of the period. The black bicorn hat, although worn according to individual taste, was as universal in the French Army as its 18th century predecessor the tricorn had been.

Grenadier companies were supposed to wear bearskin or fur caps, but because of scarcity of material this was not always possible. Despite difficulties however, the Republicans tried to continue the tradition, and contemporary evidence shows that fur caps were worn after the Revolution.

It is interesting to note that the term *"bleu"* for a recruit dates from this period, as it originated because of comparison between the still white clad regulars, and the new volunteers in blue.

31. *Infantry, 1810*

The 1793 uniform was worn by infantry at the beginning of the Empire, but it was not until after 1804 that the regulations began to be strictly enforced in detail.

The infantry coat now issued and worn by all regiments was blue with white lapels, red collar and cuffs with white piping and red epaulettes. Breeches, waistcoats and gaiters were white, although black gaiters were normally worn while on service. Shakos were supposed to be worn with this uniform, but it was not until the Imperial Decree of February 1806 that all infantry were ordered to wear them. During the campaign in Prussia most regiments had hats, and Prussian shakos were issued from captured stores. Napoleon still complained in a letter of March 1807 that manufacture must be speeded up, but it was not until 1808 that all units received them. In 1810 a new model appeared, a decree of November of that year abolishing cords, although many regiments still wore them.

This print shows a Grenadier (left) and *Voltigeur* of the Line. The Grenadier has red cords and plume, and also red lace on his shako, while the *Voltigeur* has yellow shako embellishments and yellow collar and cuffs.

Bearskin caps were still worn by some infantry grenadiers, but this was not official.

The pack, or knapsack, was now made of cow skin, and in April 1806 a greatcoat of grey or beige cloth was issued.

The musket, usually known as Model Year IX in the revolutionary calendar, was virtually the 1777 pattern and remained the standard infantry firearm throughout the period of the Empire.

A regulation of July 1806 reintroduced white uniforms, but these were only worn by a few regiments, and the idea was abandoned by 1807.

32. *Light Infantry, 1810*

The regiments of Light Infantry wore white piped blue uniforms with scarlet lapels and cuffs. Unlike the ordinary infantry they had blue breeches and short black gaiters in the Hungarian style, and as early as 1801 were further distinguished by wearing shakos before they were issued to the army in general. This headdress, with a high plume on the left side, was similar to the pattern worn by hussars at the same period.

The grenadier companies of the Light regiments were known as *Carabiniers*, and adhered to the accepted custom by wearing bearskin caps. When *Voltigeur* companies were added to light infantry in 1804, they had buff, or yellow, distinctives instead of the normal scarlet. The centre companies did not have fringed epaulettes, although these were worn by *Carabiniers* and *Voltigeurs*, in combinations of red, yellow and green.

Up to 1812 regimental differences were notable in the light infantry, but after this date an all blue jacket was universal, and *Carabiniers* had shakos in most cases, instead of bearskin caps.

This print shows a *Voltigeur* (left) and a *Carabinier*. The *Carabinier* wears the regulation blue breeches and tasselled gaiters, while the *Voltigeur* has blue trousers with a yellow stripe. His shako has yellow cords and lace; the epaulettes are green and yellow. At this period some regiments had scarlet lapels, but others were blue.

33. *Infantry, 1812*

In 1812 a completely new short jacket called a *habit-veste* was introduced. This was very similar to a jacket already worn by Polish troops, and it was first issued to the 1st battalion of each regiment. Although it was the regulation dress after 1812, the old 1804 pattern was also still in wear up to Waterloo.

The colour was still blue with white lapels, the full epaulettes now being replaced by shoulder straps, with red piping for grenadiers and yellow for *Voltigeurs.*

The 1810 shako had been ornamented by a diamond, or lozenge, shaped plate, but a new 1812 model had an eagle plate, and brass chin scales were now fitted. Company colours were displayed on small shako tufts or pompons; 1st green, 2nd blue, 3rd orange, 4th violet.

This contemporary engraving from the Martinet series shows an officer of this period wearing the black hunting boots with yellow tops so fashionable at the time.

Rank was indicated by the decoration on the epaulette strap, the size of the fringes, and whether one or two were worn, and also by the width of the gold or silver lace at the top of the shako. This is either a captain or a lieutenant, as a major would have fringed epaulettes on each shoulder.

The uniform is identical to the Infantry of the Line, but this particular print is of a veteran company with crimson lapels and silver lace.

All officers wore gorgets. The sword is the pattern known as the *épée à la mousquetaire*, which was the regulation for all infantry officers, although many variations existed.

54

34. *Infantry, 1814*

The Order of 12th May 1814, after the defeat of Napoleon, establishing the infantry of the Royal Army, stated that each regiment should be of three battalions, with six companies in each battalion. The 1st and 2nd Regiments were to be named the King's and Queen's Regiments respectively, but it appears that these names only existed on paper.

Very little was done about uniform, and the 1812 pattern was worn by all units, with the eagle shako plates replaced by one of similar shape but with a crowned oval bearing three lilies surmounted by a crown in place of the eagle. The Bourbon insignia also occupied ·all other parts of the uniform previously decorated with eagles or the letter "N". Drummers gave up their green 1812 model jackets, these being replaced by garments of similar design in royal blue.

In all other respects uniforms were unchanged and when Napoleon returned from Elba many soldiers produced their old badges which they had carefully hidden. There is little doubt however that, because of the haste and confusion of the Hundred Days, some royalist badges may have found their way into the ranks of the Napoleonic army at Waterloo. Pay books and other documents found on the battlefield certainly refer to units under their titles conferred in May 1814, and few drummers can have had 1812 jackets to change back to.

This very rare engraving, published by Basset of Paris, can be dated within a few months, as it shows the Napoleonic uniform with the first Restoration shako plate, which was discarded in March 1815, after being in use, allowing for time of manufacture, only from the middle of 1814. The unit is *Garde de Paris*, whose *Bataillons de Guerre* had fought at Friedland and in Spain.

55

35. *Departmental Legions, 1815–1820*

The Legions which replaced the infantry regiments after Waterloo were dressed in white uniforms in accordance with Bourbon tradition, as blue was reserved for Royal, or Household troops, in the Royalist infantry.

The design was however almost exactly the same as the 1812 pattern except for the colour.

Each Legion was identified by the colour of collar, lapels, and cuffs, grenadiers, fusiliers, and *Voltigeurs* were recognised by the shape and colour of their shako plumes or pompons, and the ornaments on the turnbacks of the jacket.

At first the 1812 pattern shako was worn with the Royal shako plate introduced in 1814, but a new shako was approved and worn by the Legions, which was narrower than the Napoleonic model being 215mm in diameter at the top against the 240mm of the 1812 type. A new shako plate was brought out in March 1816, and in 1818 the white cockades were made of metal instead of cloth.

This print shows a soldier of a centre, or fusilier, company of a Legion, who had flat *aigrettes* on the shako. The 1st battalion had blue, the 2nd red, the 3rd green, until 1819 when the 3rd had yellow and the 4th green. In each case the company was indicated by a brass numeral. Grenadiers and *Voltigeurs* had spherical pompons in red or yellow.

Grenadiers wore grenades on the jacket turnbacks, the fusiliers a fleur-de-lys, and *Voltigeurs* a hunting-horn (*cor-de-chasse*). The *Chasseur* battalions had a horn and a fleur-de-lys on the turnbacks.

36. *Infantry, 1822*

When the numbered infantry regiments were re-established in 1820 they were given a completely new uniform. A blue single-breasted jacket was worn with trousers instead of breeches, the trousers being blue for winter, and white for summer. Full red or yellow epaulettes identified grenadiers and *Voltigeurs* respectively, but centre companies had no fringes on their epaulettes.

At this time a new double-breasted grey overcoat was issued.

In May 1822 all 60 infantry regiments were given distinctive colours, for which purpose they were divided into groups of four, different combinations of colours of collars, cuffs, piping, and jacket turnbacks identifying the regiment. Regiments 1 to 4 were white, 5 to 8 crimson, 9 to 12 yellow, 13 to 16 rose, 17 to 20 orange, 21 to 24 light blue, 25 to 28 buff and 29 to 32 green. From the 33rd Regiment the same colours start again, but shown in a different sequence of cuffs, collar, etc.

A third pattern shako plate with the fleur-de-lys was introduced in 1821, and a new shako in 1825, grenadiers and *Voltigeurs* being distinguished by double red or yellow pompons respectively.

The Light Infantry wore the same uniform as the ordinary infantry, but they had pointed cuffs and yellow distinctives, which included the lace round the top of the shako.

In 1828 distinctive colours were abandoned and all ordinary infantry had red collars, etc., and the light infantry yellow.

This print shows a grenadier of a light infantry regiment with yellow lace and red epaulettes, in summer dress.

Colour Plate 2 (page 36). *Colour-Bearer, 1830*

This print was published in the year Louis Philippe came to the throne, and shows an officer of light infantry. The uniform is still the 1822 pattern in general style, but a notable change is that red trousers were now worn by all infantry, a custom which was to be maintained henceforth. This innovation occurred in 1829, and it has been said that it was done to give work to the dye industry, but this seems unlikely. It seems more likely that if a reason is to be found it lies in the realms of politics, as in the last months of the Bourbons the aspect of a regiment on parade was changed from blue and white, to blue, white, and red.

The shako should be the 1825 pattern, but many experiments were made in the 1830s, and variations in shape occur. A tricolour cockade replaces the white one, with the red on the outside for the first time. Double plumes indicate *élite* companies, tricolour plumes being worn by certain categories of officers and N.C.O.s.

A new shako was approved in 1837, and was issued to the 60th Regiment in July of that year. This was little different from the previous model but had less tapered sides, and was very unpopular.

The flag is a tricolour surmounted by the Gallic Cock, which was adopted in 1830 as the universal military insignia.

37. *Infantry 1841*

In the 1830s infantry went to North Africa wearing the modified 1822 designs then in use, but these were soon adapted to local conditions. This is an important print of the period, showing the 17th Light Infantry as they appeared in 1841 on return from foreign service, after having taken part in several Algerian engagements, including the capture of Constantine.

The greatcoat is still the type introduced in 1822, but the skirts have been buttoned back for easier movement, and the red trousers are tucked into the short gaiters. Cross-belts have been discarded, and instead the ammunition pouch is slung in front. The most significant feature is the headdress, known as the *casquette d'Afrique*, which was devised and worn by all troops in Algeria, and is the first appearance of the *képi*, and the origin of many later caps and shakos. This version is red cloth, with a hard leather peak. Despite the modern appearance of this soldier, his regulation dress is still unchanged, and the transformation is due entirely to active service conditions. It was about this time that the French practice of wearing greatcoats without jackets began, the uniform jacket, or coatee, which was still worn on formal occasions, is almost certainly not being worn under the coat in this case.

The musket is a flintlock, percussion weapons being introduced about 1840, and becoming general issue by 1842.

Lith de Villain

38. *Infantry, 1845*

The regulations of 1845 introduced a completely new uniform, partly in keeping with current fashion trends, but mainly because of service experience. A dark blue three-quarter length tunic was made standard for all infantry, and the equipment and side-arms were carried on a waistbelt supported by shoulder straps. The ammunition pouch was normally worn at the back, but could be attached to the front if necessary. Loops were attached to the tunic which helped to support the weight of the equipment, which included the 1833 pattern short sword in addition to a socket bayonet.

In 1843 a shako appeared based on the *casquette d'Afrique*, this was adopted by an Order of February 1844, and subsequently included in the 1845 regulations. The 1844 version had no brass plate, the regimental number being shown on the bottom band, but in March 1845 descriptions of a brass plate including a stamped number were issued. Grenadiers and *Voltigeurs* continued to wear double pompons of red and yellow, and Light Infantry had yellow lace instead of red. All shakos were supplied with black covers with painted numbers for use in bad weather.

This print shows the true 1844 shako with a scoop peak, and leather chin strap. The two chevrons on the sleeve are of red cloth and are long service stripes. The pack, referred to in the regulations as a *havre-sac*, was of fawn cow or calf skin, the roll on top is the greatcoat inside a waterproof case or rolled cover. This cover was also used to carry the tunic when the coat was worn.

60

39. *Infantry, 1849*

This print, published in 1850, from a drawing by Raffet shows the 33rd Regiment of the Line on the road to Rome. This regiment had been in Algeria from 1843 to 1848, and the artist, who was present, depicts men of their grenadier company formed up prior to marching into the city after the siege.

They are in full marching order, with waterproof covers on the shakos, which have double red grenadier pompons. Each man carries his bivouac and pole attached to his pack. Double breasted greatcoats, still grey in the regulations, but now of a blue shade, are worn, while the tunics are rolled on top of the pack.

Tin mugs are readily available, hung from buttons or belts, not only for quenching the thirst from possible streams by the roadside, but also in anticipation of the hoped-for visits at ordered halts of the *cantinière* with her cask of wine.

The 1845 equipment is now of black leather, the ammunition pouch being carried on the waistbelt at the back. The 1842 percussion musket can also be seen clearly.

Non-commissioned rank stripes were worn on the lower sleeve, one in red cloth for 1st Class Privates, two in red for Corporals; Sergeants had one gold or silver stripe, while Sergeant-Majors had two. In Light Infantry regiments 1st Class Privates and Corporals had yellow cloth stripes.

Trousers were worn over the short white gaiters on parades, but were always tucked in for marching, or on active service.

40. *Chasseurs d'Orléans—Chasseurs à pied, 1845–1859*

The uniforms of the *Chasseurs* conformed to the general infantry pattern but were different in detail.

The tunic was dark blue with white metal buttons, and yellow piping. The yellow was related to their light infantry role, but green epaulettes further distinguished them as more specifically rifle regiments, like the German *Jägers* who wore green, which was the accepted huntsman's colour in Europe. The shako was dark blue with yellow lace and piping, decorated by a green pompon with a falling green plume for full dress. No badge, or metal plate was worn on the headdress, and in fact the original 1843 shako was retained by this corps, having at the front part a double yellow cord looped round a regimental button mounted on a tricolour cockade. The battalion was identified by a metal numeral on the lower band above the peak.

Instead of the red trousers of the ordinary infantry, *Chasseurs* wore grey-blue with a thin yellow stripe, giving an all blue appearance not only unlike other French foot regiments, but contrary to the all-green conventions for such "rifle" or "huntsmen" titled units in other armies. As with Light Infantry and *Voltigeurs*, the hunting-horn, or *cor-de-chasse*, was the insignia for all *chasseur* battalions.

Officers' uniform, which was similar to the men but in finer material and with silver shako lace, buttons and epaulettes.

The *Chasseurs à pied* wore exactly the same uniform during most of the Second Empire, and continued to be the most popular and dashing units of the infantry.

41. *Cantinière, 1852*

During the Revolutionary wars women were often to be found on the battlefield giving refreshments and what medical aid they could, and it was common for such women to become officially attached to regiments. In such cases a version of the uniform was worn, and the *cantinière* or *vivandière* became an accepted institution in the French army.

Later, their functions were more precise, and they had charge of canteens, providing soldiers with extra rations for a small charge, and touring the camps and lines with liquid refreshments. During the Second Republic, and particularly during the Second Empire, the regimental *cantinières* were given real uniforms, which were in nearly every case extremely becoming versions of the regulation dress of the regiment with which they served. They paraded with their corps, and were in every sense part of the unit, normally being married to a soldier. A number of *cantinières* died on active service while trying to help wounded soldiers or taking little luxuries to the front line. One or two such casualties were sustained in the Crimea. In every case these events are known to have caused great distress and anger in the unit concerned. Obviously some of these women were hardened campaigners, but there is no doubt that most took great pride in their appearance, and if a unit was lucky enough to have a personable *cantinière* she was invariably treated as a kind of regimental mascot.

This print, published in the early 1850s, shows the infantry uniform. The short blue dress has the fashionable tight waist of the period, and is worn with a ribboned hat and red trousers. The white apron was common to all these uniforms whatever the unit, in this case light infantry piping can be seen.

42. *Infantry, 1855*

In March 1852 an Imperial Decree restored the eagle as the national emblem, and it was worn on the 1845 shakos, which were still in use. At first there was no crown on the eagle's head, but this was added in 1855, and at the same time brass chin scales replaced the leather strap. When the Light Infantry were abolished in 1854 the regiments affected changed their yellow lace for red. In 1856 a new shako appeared similar to the previous model, but now all infantry had the yellow lace previously reserved for light regiments.

The new shako was lower than the previous model and was finally issued to all units by an Order of 17th May 1856, its standardisation being confirmed by the regulations of January 1858.

This print, from a series published during the Second Empire, shows the Imperial version of the basic 1845 uniform and equipment, in parade order. The greatcoat is now carried strapped to the pack, or havre-sac. The epaulettes on the tunic could be attached to the greatcoat when it was worn, the tunic would then normally be taken off. The chain, or cord, attached to the tunic buttons is for the pricker used to clear the musket cap nipple.

This is the uniform worn by French infantry during the Crimean War, affecting the designs of British uniforms henceforth, although French fashions had been copied by other nations for some time.

64

43. *Infantry, 1861–1867*

In 1860 the infantry uniform was completely changed and the long skirted tunic gave way to a short single-breasted blue tunic called the *habit-tunique*. This was worn with very wide trousers, ending at mid-calf, with brown or fawn leather leggings occupying the space between the trousers and white gaiters. This was in fact the design worn earlier by the *Chasseurs à pied* of the Guard. Yellow was now the distinctive colour for all infantry, and this colour was on the collar and the cuff patches. Red epaulettes were worn by the grenadier companies, yellow by the *Voltigeurs*, and green with scarlet piping for the centre.

Early in 1860 the 56th Regiment paraded in the new uniform which included another new shako, this time made entirely of stout leather. The Emperor carried out a personal inspection, and on 30th March 1860 orders were given for the whole of the infantry to be issued with the new uniform and headdress.

In 1867 further alterations were made, and a double-breasted tunic with two rows of seven buttons replaced the *habit-tunique*. This, with a yellow collar, was the same for all regiments, as in January 1868 *élite* companies were abolished. The Order of December 1867 which described the new tunic, also brought in a red cloth shako with a blue band. This had two pompons, the top one being red in all cases, the smaller lower ball was of the battalion colour, and also bore the company number in brass.

Cavalry of the Line

There were 23 regiments of Heavy Cavalry when the Royal titles were abolished in 1791, the numbered regiments being increased to 27 in 1792, and reduced to 25 in 1799.

The 8th Regiment, as ex-*Cuirassiers du Roi*, already wore the cuirass, and in 1802 these began to be issued to other regiments. On 24th September 1803 the first twelve regiments were designated Cuirassiers, the 13th, 14th, 15th, 16th, 17th and 18th being turned into dragoons. The remainder were disbanded and the men absorbed into the twelve cuirassier regiments. These twelve regiments existed at the beginning of the First Empire, and were augmented by a 13th in 1809, and in 1810 the 2nd Dutch Regiment entered French Service receiving the number 14.

The two regiments of Carabiniers carried on into the Empire as separate Heavy Cavalry, and still continued under their own title when they were equipped as Cuirassiers in 1810.

Dragoons were numbered up to 18 in 1791 but were substantially increased, first by three new units in 1793, rising to 30 during the Empire. In June 1811 the 1st, 3rd, 8th, 9th, 10th and 29th Dragoons were converted to Lancers, the numbers in the Dragoon list being left vacant.

There were six regiments of *Chasseurs à cheval* originally in the old Royal Army, six more being added in 1788. By 1801 26 regiments of *Chasseurs* were in existence, and this large mounted category stood at 31 regiments in 1811. Hussars were taken over by the Republicans and given numbers up to 6, but they were increased to units up to number 14 in 1793. During the Revolutionary period there were several irregular Hussar formations, and these were used to make up the new regiments of the Line. *Les Guides de l'Armée d'Allemagne*, became the 7th Hussars, *les Hussards de la Liberté* became the 9th Hussars, *les Hussards Noirs* (or *Hussards de la Mort*) became the 10th Hussars. Other such units were absorbed by the various regular regiments.

The Hussars had been reduced in number by the beginning of the Empire, and were numbered up to 10 for some time; however, an 11th Regiment was added in 1810, being in fact the 2nd Dutch Hussars who joined the French Service in that year, and the 13th and 14th were raised in 1814.

In 1807 Polish Lancers entered French Service, and after a short period in Westphalia, rejoined the French Army as the Lancers of the Vistula Legion on 20th March 1808. In June 1811 the 1st and 2nd Vistula Lancers were incorporated into the new French Lancer Arm as the 7th and 8th *Chevau-Légers Lanciers Polonais*, Regiments 1 to 6, being titled *Chevau-Légers-Lanciers de France*. These, as we have seen, were converted dragoons. A 9th Regiment was added dressed in Polish uniform, but they were Germans, mainly from *Dragons de Hambourg*. The Polish Lancers of the Line should not be confused with the Polish Lancers of the Guard.

There were between 90 and 100 regiments of cavalry in the last campaigns of 1814, and 20,000 French horsemen were assembled for the last act at Waterloo. This formidable force suffered the same confusions as the rest of the Army until the Restoration brought new organisations.

The Order of August 1815 which disbanded the Army, authorised a new Cavalry Arm of 47 regiments. As conscription was no longer in force these all depended on volunteers, and were therefore fairly small at first with four squadrons with one company each, instead of the previous two, in the six or eight squadron Napoleonic regiments.

The Royal Cavalry of the Line consisted of one regiment of *Carabiniers*, six of Cuirassiers, ten of Dragoons, 24 of *Chasseurs à cheval* and six of Hussars. The *Carabiniers* and Cuirassiers were given Royal titles, the rest were named after regions.

These regiments continued into the service of Louis Philippe in 1830, but an Order of 12th March 1831 brought another new organisation. This established two regiments of *Carabiniers*, and ten of Cuirassiers, called Cavalry of the Reserve. Twelve dragoon and six lancer regiments were classed as Cavalry of the Line, and 14 *Chasseurs* and six hussars as Light Cavalry. They had six squadrons, each with 154 men. There had been no lancers in the Royal Army Line but the Lancers of the Royal Guard were taken into the Line in August 1830. On 19th February 1831 the first five regiments of *Chasseurs à cheval* were converted to lancers, and in the March Organisation, the *Lanciers d'Orléans* (ex-Royal Guard), were given the number 6.

Some discontent had existed since 1815 when the old *élite* companies of Line Cavalry were abolished, but Louis Philippe replaced this recognition of good soldiers by the introduction of the grade of Troopers 1st Class.

The Order of 8th December 1841 increased the cavalry by two dragoon, two lancer and three hussar regiments. The *Chasseurs à cheval* were however reduced by one as the 14th had become the

8th Lancers in 1836. *Chasseurs d'Afrique* were created in November 1831, and four regiments were included in the 1841 organisation. The 1st Regiment was raised in Algiers in March 1832, from volunteers from other regiments, and the other three in April 1832, February 1833 and December 1839 from the same source.

Three regiments of Algerian *Spahis* are listed in 1841, these native units having been raised by an Order of September 1834 as *Spahis D'Alger*, *Spahis D'Oran* and *Spahis de Bone*. In July 1845 these regiments were designated 1st, 2nd and 3rd *Spahis*.

It is interesting to note that although most of the officers were French, Arabs were admitted to the commissioned ranks as Lieutenants and 2nd Lieutenants and many of these native officers had received numerous decorations for gallantry by the mid-40s.

The 2nd Empire began with 312 squadrons of cavalry, with an extra seven regiments in the African Army. The general composition was unchanged, but there were now 12 *Chasseur* regiments, and the 9th Hussars were disbanded on 4th May 1856.

The regimental strength was normally six squadrons and in 1856 the 4th Cuirassiers return of men and horses shows 51 officers and 1,101 men with 106 officers' horses, and 798 troop horses.

All the regiments for the new Imperial Guard Cavalry were formed from the Line, and many units had their strength reduced while this was done. The two regiments of *Carabiniers* were withdrawn from the Line in 1865, one *Carabinier* Regiment appearing in the Guard in November 1865.

At the end of the War of 1870 the Cavalry were formed into composite *Régiments de Marche*, the whole being reorganised in 1871.

In 1874 there were 12 Cuirassiers regiments, 26 of Dragoons and 36 Light Cavalry including the four *Chasseur d'Afrique* regiments. Lancers disappeared from the French Army in 1870, although other regiments were issued with lances at later periods.

44. *Chasseur à cheval, 1792*

Regimental titles were abolished in 1791 but it was not until 1792 that the numbers appeared on the corners of shabraques and buttons. The helmet worn by infantry from 1791 to 1793 was adopted by *Chasseurs à cheval* in 1792, and remained their standard headdress until manufacture ceased in 1795. An inspection return for the 13th Regiment in September 1796 shows that they still had helmets, whereas other regiments were by this time wearing versions of the tapered felt cap with a cloth wing known as the *mirliton*. Until the issue of regulation shakos during the Empire, inspection returns show a marked lack of uniformity as regards headdress, and contemporary evidence indicates that each regiment followed its

68

whim, or at least that there was some inconsistency in the wearing of the various patterns.

This print shows the uniform worn up to 1804, when the dolman was replaced by a plain jacket, or *surtout*. In actual practice the change took place between 1804 and 1806 and, as with headwear, no two regiments were necessarily dressed according to the same regulation at any one time.

All *Chasseur à cheval* regiments wore green with white piping and in 1792 they were arranged in groups of three for easy distinction by colour, which was shown on collars and cuffs. The first regiment of each group had collars and cuffs of the distinctive colour, the second only the cuffs, and the third only the collar.

The colours of the 12 regiments at this time were: 1st, 2nd and 3rd—scarlet; 4th, 5th and 6th—yellow; 7th, 8th and 9th—rose; 10th, 11th and 12th—crimson.

Trumpeters still wore a full dress coat of blue with the Royal livery.

45. *Heavy Cavalry, 1800*

The heavy cavalry of the King's Army were all dressed in blue coats, white waistcoats and breeches, and black cocked hats of infantry pattern.

A variety of distinctive colours, displayed on lapels, cuffs and coat turnbacks, identified the 31 regiments. Each company had a coloured pompon on the hat; red for the 1st, blue for the 2nd, pink for the 3rd and marigold for the 4th. On active service a steel skull cap was worn under the hat.

In 1791 the uniform pattern was unaltered, but the distinctive colours were simplified and divided into four groups—scarlet, yellow, crimson and rose, the last being a shade of pink. These colours were shown on collars, cuffs and shoulder-straps, and on the tip of a black hat-plume.

Horse furniture included a blue shabraque with holster caps, and a sheepskin saddle cover with a ...

of the regimental colour.

Each man was armed with a sword, two pistols, and a musket or musketoon, carried butt down on the off-side of the horse. Officers had two pistols and a sword.

This print by Belangé shows a cavalryman about the time of the Consulate, when the artist was born, and whereas the number occupied the shabraque corners at first, a grenade, as later used by cuirassiers, is shown.

The 2nd and 3rd Cavalry distinguished themselves at Marengo, an officer of the 2nd taking an enemy colour, while two troopers of the same regiment succeeded in capturing an Austrian general.

When the first 12 regiments were converted to cuirassiers in 1803, the 13th to 18th became the 22nd to 27th Dragoons and in due course received green uniforms and brass ...

46. *Dragoons, 1810*

Dragoons, one of the oldest arms in the French service, were given green uniforms in 1763, a colour they were to wear for a hundred years. Brass helmets had been worn by Saxe's cavalry in 1745, and a version of this was issued to dragoons in 1763.

In 1791 all dragoon regiments were numbered, and recognised by the colours of their collars, lapels, cuffs, and coat turnbacks. The helmet was brass, with a brown sealskin turban, and a leather peak was now added. During the Empire the 1791 regulations were unaltered and the distinctive colours remained the same, with new combinations for the regiments raised after this date. At this time the *élite* company, i.e. the first company of the first squadron, wore bearskin caps and red epaulettes like infantry grenadiers.

The print, published during the Empire, shows a soldier of the 13th Regiment with rose distinctives carrying the firearm in the 18th century method still favoured by regiments armed with long muskets instead of carbines.

In 1812 the full tailed coat was replaced by a short jacket, and as so many regiments were now involved, distinctive colours were arranged in groups of six.

The regimental colours were 1 to 6 scarlet, 7 to 12 crimson, 13 to 18 rose, 19 to 24 yellow, and 25 to 30 *aurore*, which shows as a shade of orange.

Individual regiments within the groups were recognised by the disposition of the distinctive colour between collar, cuffs, and turnbacks.

47. *Carabiniers, 1810–1815*

The *Carabiniers* were the senior Line Cavalry regiment, and the two which existed at the beginning of the Empire wore uniforms not unlike those of the Horse Grenadiers. They had blue coats with scarlet lapels and cuffs, and both wore black bearskin caps with red plumes. At first these had no chin straps, but the Emperor noted they frequently fell off during mounted action, a seemingly obvious hazard which was rectified by the addition of brass chin scales.

In December 1809 it was decided to equip these regiments as special cuirassiers, and they were given brass helmets, and steel cuirasses

covered with brass, those of the officers being bronzed. Red uniforms were considered, but instead they received white jackets with sky-blue collars, and red epaulettes. It is interesting to note that the jacket was the short *habit-veste* type not generally issued in the army until 1812.

Both regiments were dressed the same, except that the 1st had red cuffs, and the 2nd blue.

The helmet was a departure from the cuirassier and dragoon model, as it had no skin turban but had instead a white metal band with the letter N on front, and the horse hair mane was replaced by a curved red crest in the ancient Greek style.

The *Carabiniers* fought with distinction in the battles of the Empire, but unfortunately it was an officer of the 2nd Regiment who is alleged to have deserted at Waterloo and given the British advance details of the last attacks of the Imperial Guard.

72

48. *Cuirassiers, 1812*

The only heavy cavalry regiment originally to wear the cuirass was the 8th, and early in 1802 they were given helmets of the type already worn by dragoons but of steel instead of brass and with a black skin turban. Shortly after this, the 1st Regiment was issued with helmets and cuirasses, and in October 1802 the 2nd, 3rd and 4th were also equipped in this manner. By December of the same year the 5th, 6th and 7th had been similarly treated. Although 24th September 1803 is the date usually accepted for the complete transformation of the heavy cavalry into the new Cuirassier arm, it was not until 1804 that issue of helmets and body armour had been made to all 12 regiments.

At first the old coats were worn, but red epaulettes were added, and a new sequence of distinctive colours was devised. In 1812 the short jacket became standard, and in accordance with a decree of December 1811 carbines were issued to all cuirassier regiments, while a cartridge box was worn on a white leather shoulder belt.

At first a red helmet plume was worn at all times, but the 8th Regiment lost 85 on one day's manoeuvres in 1808, and the later practice was to use them only for parades.

The long straight bladed sword with brass hilt was issued during 1802 and 1803.

This is a drawing by Carle Vernet, who also did official drawings of the 1812 regulation uniforms, and shows a trooper of this period.

2. (Page 6). *Hussars, 1810*

Hussars in Hungarian costume had been in the French service since the early 18th century, dolmans and pelisses remaining characteristic features thereafter. Only five of the six Royalist regiments passed to Republican control, as the 4th (*Conflans*) was lost to the anti-revolutionary *emigré* forces, although their 4th squadron disassociated themselves from this. Because of the removal of the 4th, the precedence had to be altered, and a new 6th Regiment was formed from the two volunteer regiments, *Liberté* and *Égalité*.

This engraving from the contemporary Martinet series of engravings, shows the uniform of the 11th Hussars, raised in 1810, according to the 1812 regulations. Pelisse, dolman, and breeches were imperial blue, while piping, collar and looping were yellow.

Fur caps are normally associated with hussars, but they were only worn by the *élite* companies of French regiments, until they too were abolished in 1812, being replaced by grenadier pattern shakos with red plumes.

Like *Chasseurs à cheval*, hussars wore various types of headgear at first and in fact were wearing shakos like light infantry before these were issued to the Army in general. At first the badge was in the form of a metal diamond, or lozenge, but eagles were later used. At no time were all the regiments absolutely consistent, and although either the diamond or the eagle ornament should have been worn between 1810 and 1814, it was equally common to find none at all.

49. *Hussars, 1822–1830*

All but the 4th Hussars wore red trousers and red shakos at this period, the one exception having sky-blue trousers and a black shako.

The pelisses were trimmed with black lambskin, and like the dolmans were of different colours according to the regiment; in all cases the collars were red, except in that of the 4th who had blue collars.

The dolman and pelisse colours were the same in each regiment. The 1st had sky blue; the 2nd maroon; the 3rd light grey; the 4th red; the 5th dark blue and the 6th green.

The sabretache was of black leather, with a brass shield bearing the royal arms and the regimental number.

The shako was a cylindrical pattern evolved from the model coming into use in 1812, but was considerably taller.

All cavalry had two types of legwear, and whereas plain red cloth, with a piping of the distinctive colour was correct, leather-reinforced garments were also worn.

These regiments were all named, and the subject of this print, published in the 1820s, is the 3rd (*Régiment de la Moselle*), which was raised in 1816.

The old 3rd Hussars of 1791 was disbanded in 1815, but they too had grey pelisses and dolmans, a dress distinction which began with the Esterhazy Regiment raised in 1764.

All the regiments of Hussars took part in the 1823 Spanish campaign, their smart appearance and great *élan* doing much to remind all concerned of the existence of a new French Army.

74

50. *Chasseurs à cheval, 1831*

The uniforms of the *Chasseurs* changed frequently over the years, and only the colour of their jackets and hunting horn insignia remained constant. In 1816 they wore green lapelled jackets, but in 1822 these had Hussar-type frogging on the breast. Shakos were black with black plumes tipped with the distinctive colour of the regiment.

Further changes were made in 1831, and a single-breasted jacket with red epaulettes was worn with red trousers reinforced with black leather. The shako was very tall at this period and had a hanging black plume.

This print by Eugène Lami, published in 1831, shows details including the red shako lines; an insurance against loss should the headdress fall off while riding. The piece of leather at the back of the shako was originally a moveable neck cover, but at this time, in other armies as well as the French, it was a fixture, and appears to have acted as a strengthener.

Shakos were later replaced by fur hussar caps, these being the regulation headdress in 1845; at the same time the red epaulettes were changed to white.

The 1822 pattern carbine was suspended by a ring and swivel from the shoulder belt which carried the cartridge box.

The 4th Regiment were in Spain in 1823, and at Alcaras a detachment of 20 men under a lieutenant, charged 40 Spanish dragoons, who, in the words of the official report, were tumbled or "somersaulted" into flight.

In 1831 the 4th were transformed into lancers, and a new 4th *Chasseurs* were raised from elements of the 9th.

51. *Carabiniers, 1831*

The Order of May 1814 retained two regiments of *carabiniers*, now having the title of *Carabiniers de Monsieur*, but after Waterloo only one regiment of four squadrons was retained.

White breeches were retained for full dress and leather reinforced trousers were worn on service, but the general Napoleonic aspect remained. The cuirass was still steel, plated with brass of a bronze coloured hue, but the front plate was now decorated with a sunburst, bearing the badge of the Comte d'Artois.

In addition to the white jacket worn since 1810 a second undress coat of sky blue was now also issued.

In 1825 it was decided to re-form the two regiments, and they appeared in the new cavalry organisations of 1831, when this print was published. They now lost the traditional white uniforms, both units wearing sky blue in all orders of dress. This uniform had scarlet epaulettes, grey trousers with blue piping, and yellow or buff belts. The brass-plated cuirass had a Gallic Cock on the front plate, the two regiments being distinguished by the placing of red and sky-blue cuffs, collars, collar piping, cuff patches, and turnback ornaments.

A very similar appearance was kept until the regiment of *Carabiniers* were included in the Imperial Guard in 1866. In 1871 this unit was amalgamated with the 11th Cuirassiers.

52. *Dragoons, 1835*

This print, published in 1835, shows the dragoons as they appeared at the end of the Restoration period, and the beginning of Louis Philippe's reign.

Jackets were green with distinctive colours shown on lapels, cuffs and collars, in groups of four regiments—1 to 4 were rose, 5 to 8 were yellow, and 9 and 10 crimson.

Trousers were grey with piping of the distinctive colour, but these were later changed to plain red cloth for dismounted wear, and red cloth reinforced with leather for mounted duty.

An order of July 1821 replaced the helmet with curved crest, which had been adopted in 1815, with a completely new model, but this does not appear to have been issued until some years later, some records giving the date as 1825.

The new headdress is shown in this print, and was brass for dragoons, and steel for cuirassiers, without a turban and with a horse hair brush on top of the crest, a form of decoration never used on any other French helmet design. In 1826 squadrons were identified by the colour of a ball placed at the base of the plume. The 1st squadron was blue, the 2nd crimson, the 3rd green, the 4th sky blue, the 5th rose and the 6th yellow.

At this period the 1822 pattern sword was carried, which unlike the previous heavy cavalry weapon, had a curved blade. Dragoons wore this uniform during the expedition to Belgium in 1831.

53. *Chasseurs d'Afrique, 1840*

An early representation of the corps in a series of prints by Lalaisse showing uniforms between 1840 and 1848.

The full-skirted tunic was sky blue with yellow distinctive colours; this print represents the 1st Regiment with yellow collar and cuffs. Brass shoulder scales were worn on this coat, and a cartridge box was carried on a white shoulder belt.

A notable feature was the wide red breeches with black leather false boots attached to the lower leg, a garment not introduced for cavalry in general until 1854.

At this period the regiment was sometimes referred to as *Chasseurs Lanciers d'Alger*, and a Polish *czapska* was the full dress headgear, although a red *casquette d'Afrique* with a sky-blue band was also worn. It is sometimes thought that this lancer appearance was dropped after a few years, but the regulations of 1846 still describe the Polish cap. By the Second Empire, however, only a shako, or *casquette*, is mentioned, and the light cavalry sword, rifle, and pistol were the only weapons. The shako had a pompon with different colours for each squadron, and in 1858 all regiments had yellow collars, cuffs, and piping. In 1863 the single breasted tunic was replaced by a dolman with black loops, or *brandebourgs*, on the chest.

White cloaks were now worn, and white covers fitted over the shako, or *casquette*, giving these units a very dashing appearance.

54. *Lancers, 1845–1853*

When six French dragoon regiments were converted to lancers in 1811, they did not adopt Polish dress but continued to wear their green dragoon jackets. At the same time their own brass helmets had the manes and front tufts removed, to be replaced by a curved black crest. This use of existing uniform is mentioned in the records of the 4th Lancers, ex 9th Dragoons, although modifications were made such as the issue of Hungarian breeches and boots.

After Waterloo, the lance became popular, and most armies dressed troops so armed in the Polish manner, but except for the one Guard regiment the Restoration Cavalry had no lancers.

When Louis Philippe re-created them they followed the now accepted fashion, and wore a uniform which continued with little change into the Second Empire.

The blue jackets of the first four regiments had yellow lapels, the other four having red lapels. A rather complicated system of colours variously disposed between cuffs, collars and jacket turnbacks identified individual regiments.

Epaulettes were white in all cases, the *czapska* was blue with lace and piping of the main distinctive of yellow or red.

This Lalaisse lithograph of 1853 represents the 2nd Regiment with yellow lapels, collar and cuffs. The mounted man wears leather reinforced *pantalon basane*, while the dismounted figure illustrates the red cloth trousers, in this case with blue piping.

Lances were of ash wood with a triangular steel point.

55. *Chasseurs à cheval, 1853*

Up to 1848 the *Chasseurs* wore their 1831 uniforms, but with hussar caps, but just at the end of Louis Philippe's reign they adopted the now standard sloping shako as worn by the infantry and other arms. Regiments were organised by series for distinctive colours—1st orange, 2nd yellow, 3rd red. In 1853 the uniform was completely altered, and the single-breasted jacket gave way to a green dolman of hussar pattern with 18 black loops on the chest in three rows with white metal buttons. The headdress now became a very distinctive hussar cap, but not of fur, but of curled lamb's wool dyed

black. This had a brass chin chain, and was decorated with a green and red plume. This illustration from a Lalaisse print dated 1853, shows the new false-booted red trousers, in this case with a double green stripe, which was then the fashion becoming much more common. The shabraque was green with a red border, and a hunting horn badge was embroidered on the corners in red cloth. Belts were white, according to regulations, and French cavalry do not seem to have favoured black belts even for regiments of this type.

The characteristic method of carrying the sword at attention is shown here, with the elbow back, and the hilt on the hip.

56. *Dragoons, 1854–1867*

This print, from a series by de Moraine published in 1859, shows Dragoons in the uniform they wore until 1867.

The brass helmet with a leopard skin turban was a return to the First Empire fashion, and in 1840 had replaced the 1825 model.

In 1854 leather-reinforced red trousers were finally replaced by the rather clumsy wide red breeches with false black leather boots, which had already been worn by *Chasseurs d'Afrique* for some time. Jackets were green with red epaulettes, the very large lapels of the previous régime still being a feature.

The 12 regiments were divided into three groups of four for purposes of identification. The first group had white as its distinctive colour, the second yellow and the third red. The first two regiments of each group had collars of the distinctive colour, the other two had green collars. The second and fourth regiments of each group had cuffs of the distinctive colour, the others were green. All four regiments of each group had lapels of the distinctive colour.

Dragoons, with their dual role as mounted and foot troops, were armed with a long arm instead of a carbine, which they still carried butt down in a bucket on the off side of the horse.

In 1867 an important change occurred, and the traditional green jacket was exchanged for a single-breasted plain blue tunic. Red epaulettes were still worn, but the new distinctive colour of white for all dragoons was worn on the collar, and cuff patches.

This shows a soldier of the second group with yellow plastron-shaped lapels. Incomplete colouring of the cuffs on the print prevents specific identification, but because of the green collar it is either the 7th or 8th Regiment.

82

57. *Hussars, 1859*

In 1845 hussar shakos were of the now characteristic type associated with the French Army, the rest of the uniform developing slowly until the end of the reign of Napoleon III.

Pelisses and dolmans were the same colour in each regiment, except in the case of the 8th which had a white pelisse and a sky-blue dolman. The other regiments had the traditional colours such as the brownish maroon of the 2nd, and grey of the 3rd.

The cuffs of the 1st, 3rd, 5th, 6th and 7th were red, the 2nd, 4th and 8th sky-blue. Trousers and shakos were the same colour as the cuffs except for the 7th which had green shakos, and the 2nd which had red trousers. Buttons were white metal for the first six regiments, the others being brass.

This print, published just before the 1860 regulations, shows the full dress of the period. Little had changed since the previous régime, except for the wide breeches. In 1860 or 1861, black hussar caps of lamb's wool replaced the shakos, and all regiments had red breeches with piping of the dolman colour. About this time pelisses were only worn in full dress, and the *Annuaire Militaire* of 1863 does not mention them at all. The dismounted figure on the right only wears the dolman.

The 1st and 8th regiments had sky-blue tunics with six rows of white loops in 1867, but the old fully looped dolman, as shown here, was still in use in 1870, with a *képi* on active service instead of the hussar cap.

83

58. *Cuirassier, 1860*

This print from the 19th-century history of the regiment, shows a private of the 4th Cuirassiers in the uniform worn from 1854 to about 1860.

The helmet is the 1854 version of the 1840 model, cuirassiers now having a red front tuft, while dragoons had black. The ball at the base of the plume was of the squadron colour, in this case blue, indicating the first squadron. The turban is of black seal-skin, the horsehair mane, as in all 1840 type helmets, issuing from the extreme rear of the brass crest.

The jacket was blue with red epaulettes, and in this case a long service chevron in red cloth is worn on the upper arm, while a 1st Class private's stripe can be seen beneath the white gauntlet.

Wide red breeches in this case with blue piping were now standard cavalry dress, the false boots fitting over the actual footwear. The shabraque is blue with white edging, and the regimental number was carried on the corner, and on the valise ends.

The sword is the straight-bladed 1854 pattern, and pistols were the only firearms carried.

On 14th December 1859, the short jacket was replaced by a blue tunic, whose skirts were buttoned back to show red lining. This actual change took place during 1860 and 1861; otherwise the general aspect remained unaltered until 1870.

The 4th were raised in 1643, as the Queen's, later the Queen Mother's Regiment, and kept their number throughout their history from the time they received it in 1791.